The New Principal

The New Principal

Surviving Your First Year as Educator in Charge

Margaret Carter

ROWMAN & LITTLEFIELD
Lanham • Boulder • New York • London

Published by Rowman & Littlefield
An imprint of The Rowman & Littlefield Publishing Group, Inc.
4501 Forbes Boulevard, Suite 200, Lanham, Maryland 20706
www.rowman.com

6 Tinworth Street, London SE11 5AL, United Kingdom

Copyright © 2020 by Margaret Carter

All rights reserved. No part of this book may be reproduced in any form or by any electronic or mechanical means, including information storage and retrieval systems, without written permission from the publisher, except by a reviewer who may quote passages in a review.

British Library Cataloguing in Publication Information Available

Library of Congress Cataloging-in-Publication Data

Names: Carter, Margaret, 1956– author.
Title: The new principal : surviving your first year as educator in charge / Margaret Carter.
Description: Lanham : Rowman & Littlefield, [2020] | Includes bibliographical references. | Summary: "This book leads principals through an examination of themselves and their motivation. It takes an unflinching look at the nature of today's principalship at all levels."—Provided by publisher.
Identifiers: LCCN 2020012604 (print) | LCCN 2020012605 (ebook) | ISBN 9781475855968 (cloth) | ISBN 9781475855975 (paperback) | ISBN 9781475855982 (epub)
Subjects: LCSH: First year school principals. | Educational leadership. | School management and organization.
Classification: LCC LB2831.6 .C39 2020 (print) | LCC LB2831.6 (ebook) | DDC 371.2/011—dc23
LC record available at https://lccn.loc.gov/2020012604
LC ebook record available at https://lccn.loc.gov/2020012605

To my first teachers, my parents, Leroy Alexander and Lucy Alexander; and my extended family, many who were also teachers and principals. If it were not for them and their example of being a part of a community while helping to educate it, this book would not exist.

To all the teachers, principals, and auxiliary personnel who work tirelessly day after day in the sometimes difficult and chaotic environment of struggling schools. Thank you for your dedication to our children. It is my hope that this book will assist future principals in their effort to create a positive learning environment in their own school.

To Carlie Wall for her assistance in preparation of the manuscript.

To my family who support me with love and encouragement every day.

Contents

Preface		ix
1	Know the School	1
2	Know the Staff	15
3	Informal Leaders	27
4	Know the Community	33
5	Know the Goals of the District and School	39
6	Know Yourself	45
7	Discipline	55
Conclusion		73
References		75
About the Author		77

Preface

Why I wrote this book . . .

I'd spent many years working with students, became ill, and decided to go into management—after all, managers use different skills, and I could now sit behind a desk, run meetings, organize, and dispense orders from my office. The employees, in this case, teachers, could joyfully do as I instructed them to do and our school would take off—win all kinds of awards, and we'd all live happily ever after.

Oh, how mistaken and misguided was I. Of course, my frustrated boss brought in a "consultant" who talked with all the staff. I knew the outcome would be bad but was hoping for a different result. The consultant came into my office, took my hand, and said, "They have declared war on you!" I broke down in tears—not from being sad or mad (at least not totally) but from gratitude. I thought, finally I have the answer—the answer to whispering in the halls, horrible relationships with "my" staff, and disrespectful rebelliousness coming from these professionals. Unfortunately, he didn't mention how to get things going in a better direction, but rushed out to catch his flight.

How would I fix all of this? I had read books on "How to be a better boss"—none of which helped me—they all focused on being tough, driven, single-minded, and all the other traits of bossmanship. I had all these traits in spades—why was I failing? I rushed around the school, clipboard in hand, making notes—I had much to "fix." My boss tried to help—mentioning in passing that my relationships with the staff were bad.

What to do? I was not—am still not—a natural at chummy conversations, casual gossip, and other girlfriend types of behavior. Is that what she meant? Another consultant said, "Throw a brick in your wagon—slow down, mosey around as if everything is just fine, you haven't a care in the world. Paste a smile on your face and greet everyone—no matter how you feel." Get rid of the clipboard. Work on your memory—you can make notes later. Right now, when people see you, they feel afraid—like something's wrong—somebody's in trouble.

Over the next few months, with each new assignment (you didn't think they'd keep me in that job, did you?), I started using some of the tips. With nothing to lose, practicing daily, I used these traits, and things slowly began to improve. Not because of any magic bullets, but from showing genuine interest in my team—taking the time to get to know people, their needs, wants, and desires. In other words, I had to change myself. One final thing that I read advised that I "always do repair"—(relationships). If a careless exchange or misunderstanding happens, go to the person and make it right. Wow—that was the hardest thing to do. Aren't bosses always right? Don't teammates have to come to me formally to air their grievances? Ha! The parking lot conversations are much more effective (and fun!). Hadn't I learned about forgiveness? Yes, but this is more than forgiveness, it is acknowledging that the other person is valuable to you and you want to talk it out—make it right. You (boss) need them (employees)—more than they need you.

This may sound like a plan for the inmates to take over the asylum, but take my word for it—it worked for me. I am not the boss, I am just another team member, here to bear my share of the burden, working alongside you, so that our (not my) team, and therefore, students can be successful.

Chapter One

Know the School

Want to be a successful principal? Knowing the characteristics of your school is step one. In order to be effective, principals must consider an enormous number of factors about their assigned school. It's tempting, but don't jump in with both feet before taking the time to think. What will you think about? Think about the reality of your school situation. Not what you remember from when you were in school, or what you wished for and fantasized about or hoped for during your time in graduate school, but what is actually in front of you.

Although you may not have all the information you need on your first day (usually two weeks before teachers arrive), try to get as much information about your school as you possibly can. However, don't let the time crunch scare you. Each school is unique, although all schools have many things in common. Here are only a few of the basics you should think seriously about and analyze before you choose your furniture and decide on colors for your office.

- What type of school have you been assigned to?
- How large is the staff?
- What other administrative teams are there?
- What kind of neighborhood is the school located in?
- What parent groups are there?
- Is there a staff union?
- What are the sources of income for your school?
- Are there resources that can be accessed?
- How does the school function within the neighborhood?
- Does the school have a history of constant crisis or is it a calm oasis of learning?

Asking and getting answers to these questions (as soon as possible) can lead to success for the new principal. Thoughtful observation and consideration of these questions takes time. But it's time well spent. Block in time on your schedule just to think. Spending your valuable time being busy with constructing schedules and outlining programs at this point will not lead to success. The successful administrator will calmly and patiently wait for a team of teachers or other stakeholders to help formulate plans and schedules.

Find out who was involved in scheduling during the previous year and try to make contact with the persons involved. You can work with this person or team to set a specific time to plan. Do *not* try to do it all yourself. Not even a draft. The best thing you can do is jot down talking points, questions, and ideas. Don't share proposals for change too prematurely. Be cautious with ideas. Word can get around that you "want it this way," because remember, your team is gathering information about you, too.

It is tempting to do as much as possible "in advance" because there truly is a lot "to do." This is particularly true in "high-challenge" schools. But unilateral plans, plans that you've thought of in your own mind, are failure plans. The school is like a family. In well-functioning families, each member has the other members' best interest at heart. A family is a closed system. No one is going to come in from outside that family and fix the problems for the family. The principal must find a way to develop or enhance a close relationship with the entire school family or team.

The impact of a principal cannot be underestimated in "high-challenge" schools. As Martin Haberman discusses regarding the principal's impact, "Recent research has shown that urban school principals have an even greater impact on student achievement than principals in less challenging schools. The constructive direction of a superior school leader is not limited to academics but has far-reaching consequences on teacher performance and turnover. Additionally, many studies argue the positive connection between quality principals and student academic outcomes since principals impact various student outcomes beyond test scores" (Haberman quoted in Stafford and Jackson 2016, 66).

If the administration consists of several assistant administrators, the need for team closeness multiplies exponentially. Dysfunctions within your team will only grow. Your job is to make sure your team stays on the same page, and that you are not unwittingly growing factions.

Conversely, fostering good feelings and developing open communication will only strengthen the team. This is not the time to go along and "tolerate" neutrality or accept lukewarm relationships. There needs to be a virtual love fest among administrators. Go for building unbreakable bonds between the members. Having a willingness to learn from others and an open mind can help a new principal find success and create lifelong positive relationships and even friendships. At the very least, openness and honesty will help avoid the principal developing a negative image.

A negative image, which is often obvious to everyone (but the principal), can make for a very long and frustrating school year. A negative image that goes unaddressed can ruin entire careers in educational leadership. A wise principal will make every effort to learn and keep learning while doing the job. Learn about emotional intelligence or consult with an image expert to help you get a better view of yourself and your interactions with others. With this in mind, spend time considering and analyzing the school situation. Focus on solutions, and remember to bring others along with you. You'll better enjoy the ride you take, not alone, but with others!

Personal Experience

I had been assigned to a tiny school located in a rural setting. After spending my entire teaching and administrative career in large city schools, I was failing. Big time. I had one friend on the staff. The other teachers were either mad at me for making changes or neutral cautiously because they were new and needed the support of other more seasoned teachers. Almost the entire staff had taught together for many years in this isolated location, and many lived in the immediate area. After three long years of struggle, my supervisor hired two consultants who polled and interviewed the staff. Their conclusion, as one said: "The staff has declared war on you." That one phrase was a wake-up call I needed.

I immediately began to evaluate my behavior, which was "nice"—courteous but standoffish and dictatorial. Without reading or researching relationships (which I should have done), I started to really listen to people and changed the way I went about my job. No, I was still far from perfect, but this realization changed me and helped me to learn and grow. I had thought I had it all together with my near perfect grade point average, and quickly gaining advancement. I thought I was ready, but I learned that book smart does not equal or overcome people ignorance.

Whatever your assignment, remember, relationships do matter. The job of principal is complex and a huge responsibility, but it is ultimately about people.

TO WHAT TYPE OF SCHOOL HAS THE PRINCIPAL BEEN ASSIGNED?

Obviously, there is a difference between early childhood, elementary, middle, and high school sites. Each kind of school has its own unchangeable elements, such as age group. Spend time evaluating exactly how the school functions. Include as many programs as you can think of. You may review past schedules and memos or discuss items with your secretary or an assistant administrator. He or she will know, well, basically everything.

This exercise will help you to see the overall school and how it functions. It will help you to determine the overall structure and help you to budget your time for each task, program, or department. If you taught at one level, such as middle school, and are assigned to another level, say elementary, spend time reading about current issues at the level to which you are assigned. Don't rely on your memories about your time at that particular level or school. Yes, the basics are the same (layout, staff, programs), however, much will have changed over the years about students, teachers, customs, and so on at every school setting.

HOW LARGE OR SMALL IS THE STAFF?

Is your staff large or small? Is it a homogenous group where teachers all teach the same subject, or grade level? Or is the staff heterogeneous with a mix of subjects or grade levels?

Personal Experience
Are small staffs or tiny schools easier? Please don't believe this. Before being promoted to principal, I had been an assistant principal at the largest elementary school in the district with over eight hundred students, forty-five teachers, and twenty-five non-certified staff. Moving to the smallest school in the district, with one hundred students and one teacher per grade level, I thought it would be an easy assignment with time to spare. Unfortunately, this tiny school scored lowest in the district in reading and math. I set out to put things in order so I could focus on the student's academic needs.

When I asked about programs, committees, and schedules, the lead teacher replied, making a circular motion with her hands, "We all do everything!" What? How is that possible? Well I found out how possible it was! Determined to do as I had successfully done at the large school, I plowed ahead and tried to form teams (one teacher and myself). After all, a team of two is still a team. It would be her responsibility to get the word out about what "we" had decided. Well word indeed did get around about everything we'd decided, the informal leaders took over, parking lot meetings were held, and the plans exploded—right in my face.

In a large school, with many programs and teams, the principal's job is, in many ways easier. Because of the sheer number of people available to do the work, the labor and the leadership is distributed. The principal's task is to find a balance between having enough teams so that everyone can function within their best capacity and having too many teams where their goals, activities, and responsibilities become crossed, resulting in confusion. More discussion on staff teams can be found in chapter 2 on staff.

WHAT ADMINISTRATIVE TEAMS ARE THERE?

After teacher teams are identified and established, that leaves the most important team you will be in charge of: your own administrative team. Different school levels require different strategies for dividing administrative team assignments. At the high school level, there usually are two or more assistant principals. Middle schools operate much like high schools. Elementary schools usually have one principal and one assistant principal. Meet with the personnel involved, ask everyone to write or tell their experience and perceived area of strength. Explore strengths and weaknesses and the time involved for each task. Ask about preferences, and try to come to a consensus. Of course, the principal has final say in assignments. Other things to explore are before- and after-school duties, night ball games and events, and emergency contingency plans.

If you can choose the members of your own administrative team, lucky you! This can be a rare but good place to start. However, be very cautious—choosing people who look like you, function like you, think like you, and have fun like you can be counterproductive. It is best to select a wide variety of people on your team, especially to reflect the diversity of your staff and students. Diversity goes far beyond racial and gender demographics. Principals need people who are different from themselves—in temperament, academic expertise, leadership style, and other personality traits.

If there are staff assigned to your team who were there before you arrived, or who were assigned for another reason without your input, it is in your best interest to get to know these professionals and make a special effort to discover what their strengths are. Finding a place for this person and exploring assignments that fit their skill set will help to form an effective team. Keeping an administrator whom you did not choose out of the loop and on the margin will not help you or the school.

What if you have an extra team member that you are having a hard time finding a place for on your team? Having a "lost" staff member is a waste of talent. Every person is needed in today's school. You don't want anyone just hanging out there with nothing to do. The person with little to do could, at best, carry out assignments in an unenthusiastic, uninformed, doubtful manner, or worse, secretly, unintentionally, or even openly undermine your efforts.

How do you craft a good administrative team? Meet with your team frequently at first, then possibly—hopefully—less frequently as the school year progresses. It would be a good idea to meet with your team each morning and each evening, especially in high-challenge schools.

The principalship of a large school, or any school in any setting, is not to be taken lightly. Only the most serious candidates need apply. With the right teams in place, your school will have a greater chance of success for its students, teachers, and you.

Personal Experience

One year I was assigned as assistant principal to a high school. It was late in the summer when I got the assignment, so late that school was scheduled to begin in a few weeks. It was clear, to me at least, that I was the last one to be placed. Nevertheless, this was an exciting time for me. Early in my career, I had been a teacher in a high school setting for many years. I remembered how it was to be with students who were right on the edge of beginning their adult lives. I knew I could make an impact on them directly, or indirectly through establishing and supporting various programs. When I arrived to meet the principal, he knew my name and a little about my background, but only as a principal in an elementary setting. The administrative team had already been established and given assignments by grade levels.

All the "extra" or non-academic assignments had already been given. The offices were full. It was quite obvious that the principal didn't know what to do with me. So, I spent the entire year being moved from office to office, from assignment to assignment, "helping out" here and there. After spending an entire year "in limbo," I was moved back to an elementary position, where I spent my last two years before retirement. I had gone full circle but had learned so much about team building during the trip. My personal pledge was to never put another professional in that position.

WHAT KIND OF NEIGHBORHOOD IS THE SCHOOL LOCATED IN?

The influence of the community informs every part of the student's lives and largely determine how they show up for school. Is the school located in an affluent area or are parents struggling daily to survive? Are there businesses, libraries, and community agencies in the area, or is your school in a rural farm community? The school may have four walls, classrooms, and a roof, but the community may as well be inside your building.

Personal Experience

My first principalship was in a school that was located in a semi-rural location on the farthest edge of the city. In fact, my colleagues used to joke that "you have to take a lunch to drive there." The majority of the homes were on at least one acre, and many farms and farm animals were in the area. The population was aging, with grandparents raising grandchildren. There was also a community garden across the street where the sponsor supplied us all with watermelons, squash, and other seasonal produce. At dismissal one warm spring day, students and bus duty teachers were all standing outside on the north side of the building, waiting for the bus to arrive. Parents in idling cars were waiting for their children. Suddenly, something to the west caught our attention, as we squinted into the afternoon sun, a horse and rider were galloping toward us at a good pace. Before we knew it, horse and rider had scooped up two children, almost without stopping, and rode off to the east. That's when I knew I was in a very special rural school.

WHAT PARENT GROUPS ARE THERE?

Parents will always have a vested interest in their child's schooling. Their interest may be active or passive, but you always have their most precious investment in your care. In most schools there is an established parent organization. Some parents help out at school individually, while other parents desire a more organized approach and like to participate in group support of the school. Many parents limit their involvement to their own child's particular interest, for example band, sports booster clubs, or academic competitions.

This is no problem, except when parents get overly zealous in defending their child's place in these activities. Principals should support the coach or sponsor as they resolve issues, as they are much closer to the problem than the principal. If the staff sponsor is found to be mistaken or wrong, meet with him or her privately and encourage a resolution for the good of the program. If the parent still has an issue, or comes to you without the knowledge of the coach or sponsor, be sure to request that person's presence at the meeting.

Fortunately, there are parents in *all* schools who are concerned about the school that their children attend and will do all they can to help out. Unfortunately, some parents tend to misunderstand the legalities of parent organizations and believe that business can be handled in any way they feel is appropriate. It is the principal's job to assist parents in understanding the proper procedures, best practices, and legalities when handling money from fund-raising activities.

Be cautious about parent organizations. You want to encourage parent engagement in your school. There is a sharp line between fund-raising for the school and its students and using the school for parents' personal slush fund or as a bank for short-term loans. Note: the national Parent Teachers Association is a separate organization, and schools may not use the term *PTA* without membership and approval from the national organization. If a school wants to establish its own parent organization, this is fine. Only keep in mind about what the organization is named. Monitor their activities from a healthy distance, and help when asked.

The principal must understand his or her role in the parent organization as well. In most states, the principal's role is strictly "hands off." Do not sign checks or place yourself as an owner on a parent organization bank account. These items are usually covered in principals' training meetings or at a special training provided by the school district and/or state department of education. Meet with your immediate supervisor before you have to meet with a judge regarding parent organization funds. Although legally the principal may not be held liable for parent organizations and their misuse of funds, incidents of improper handling of money will always reflect badly on the principal.

IS THERE A FORMAL STAFF UNION OR TEACHER ORGANIZATION?

Schools with strong and active unions will function and focus differently than schools without union influence. There will be a union handbook. Become thoroughly familiar with this legally binding agreement. Some staff members seem to hide behind union rules to mask their ineffectiveness in the classroom while preserving their right to remain employed. Make certain that you have introduced yourself to the union representative and the teacher representative before you have to meet them in a more contentious setting.

The role of the teachers union has changed since the 1970s when unions were new. Teacher unions were formed, in part, due to unfair practices that were in place. Such practices included incompetence, negligence, or ignorance on the part of some school districts or administrators. There was also a need to outline standard practices of employment and working conditions within schools. Over time, school unions became powerful, at times more powerful than the district itself. This resulted in incompetent staff members who were able to remain on the job, resulting in the suffering of children's education. The relationship between unions and schools became adversarial.

At this writing, teacher unions have shifted toward working with teachers in conjunction with the administration for the good of both parties. It is a much more collaborative process, which helped children's education.

KNOW THE SCHOOL'S FINANCES AND SOURCES OF INCOME: FEDERAL, STATE, LOCAL, SPECIAL

All money is not the same. Federal money buys certain items and can be used only a certain way; state money buys teachers and books; local (district) money usually buys items particular to your school. Special money is grant money or comes from sources that you have procured on your own. There is a department or person assigned to help you with using your funds; although much of it you will not "see."

The district or state education department will spend money for you and pass the resources to your school. Should you have money that you have complete control over, establish an advisory team. Remember that "people may not always have their way, but they will have their say." The school district or state education department will help you to stay in compliance with the guidelines that come with school money.

ARE THERE EXTERNAL RESOURCES THAT CAN BE ACCESSED?

Some schools are fortunate to have generous donors with deep pockets and have to choose how to use the additional funding. This situation brings a set of problems and issues of its own. There may be strings attached or qualifications that must be met to receive the funding. Be sure these conditions are legal, moral, and ethical and for the ultimate good of all students and the school in its entirety.

Other schools struggle with minimal funding and have to scrape and beg for additional funds. These principals find they must spend time exploring new funding sources and learn to apply for grants. It is illegal for principals to procure loans for their school. This leaves grants—public and private. Grant writing has become much easier than it was in the past. Once a grant has been written and approved, grant writing becomes more attractive and easier. Become an expert information (data) gathering machine. You'll learn which data pieces are most often asked for and you will begin to gather information as it becomes available throughout the years. Establish a file for achievement data so it will be at your fingertips at a moment's notice. Learn to analyze and connect the dots to an increase in student achievement, attendance, or whatever your goal may be.

Most grantors simply want to know about your school: its students, challenges, and needs. They need to understand how you plan to tackle the situation and how you plan to spend the resource (not always money) they will give you. Once you win and receive your grant, grant writing will become a habit; just another part of what you do.

HOW DOES THE SCHOOL FUNCTION WITHIN THE NEIGHBORHOOD?

When neighbors or community organizations think of your school, what is their first thought? Is the school seen as a Monday-through-Friday institution where kids are dropped off at eight o'clock and picked up at three and weekends are silent? Or is your school a fully functioning community school, open on weekends, complete with basic health care, where you can get vaccinations and basic health screenings? Is there a staff of social workers who are there to assist families? Is your school's library open after hours for parents to bring kids for checkout or story time?

How about its availability for constituents to pay nominal fees to host gatherings, community sporting events, or other activities? Maybe your school is an official storm shelter. All these factors influence how people perceive your school, and by extension, how they see you. If you feel that something is missing from your school's image, work with your staff to develop a short (five questions) survey to find out how your community feels about your school. Contact your district's public information office. They may already have this data on file for you to review.

DOES THE SCHOOL HAVE A HISTORY OF CONSTANT CRISIS OR IS IT A CALM OASIS OF LEARNING?

When people think of your school, what is the first thing that comes to their minds? Is it the big fight that burst out last week and the police had to respond? Or are there pleasant memories of young people playing soccer in the open playground on a weekend morning?

A principal will function and focus on issues much differently at a chaotic school than at a school in a more stable environment. Keeping gang violence out of school requires a different skill set than keeping parents from overstepping their boundaries within the classroom. A word of caution for administrators in unsettled schools: Placing too much focus on negative, nonacademic behaviors will turn the school into a prison. In this type of environment, the goal is to warehouse students until they can be further incarcerated. Is this what you want your school to be?

To address this issue, you'll need to consider making changes to the traditional way that students are identified for advanced programs. Make a special effort to identify students who might fall through the cracks between academics and athletics. These students may be successful in one of the special academic programs or an activity that does not involve sports ability to get involved.

There may be, and probably are, barriers to participating in extracurricular activities, such as transportation needed in order to stay after school or to come in early. Instead of holding on to traditional qualifications to participate, pave a way for these students to join. An educator's mission is to develop students, not to capitalize on what is already there. This kind of guidance is what many children and their families are seeking from the adults at school.

WHAT ARE THE CUSTOMS OR TRADITIONS OF THE SCHOOL?

Finding out about the important events at school can begin with your personal, firsthand experience. If you attended the school or lived in the area, you definitely have the advantage. Examine the budget to see how and where the money is spent. Look at the activities schedule and the weekly calendars.

Establish a solid schedule of activities. Avoid changing major activities if at all possible. Additional unexpected activities can place a burden on everyone involved. Canceling activities can lead people to feel something is going wrong and to wonder why. Learn to defend your schedule by vetoing almost all impromptu activities unless it is an emergency. This applies to schoolwide activities. Individual classrooms of course, have much more leeway, although the goal is to still have a steady, reliable list of activities. Reach out to each department to find out what they have planned. Sponsors of these activities will usually ask for a meeting to discuss their needs for the year well in advance, before the budgeted money is already allocated.

Is the school's focus on academics, athletics, or the arts? Or are individual activities the focus—the prom, sports royalty, and yearbook? Many districts have assigned their schools a focus, and you will be expected to excel in that focus. The principal who wants to change the mission of the school is in for a major battle. Not because these programs are wrong, but traditions at any school or in any organization is extremely difficult to change.

Slow, tiny modifications are many times the best way to institute change over a few years. Have a solid, justifiable reason for the change; get people to see a different perspective; and hopefully staff or community members will take up the cause for you. Avoid having people change just because "the principal said so." Starting a new program helps move change along, as there is a limit on folks' time, energy, and money.

Personal Experience
During my teaching career, I had chosen to work at the district's only alternative education center. The center was for students who were either young parents or expectant mothers or students who needed credits due to being expelled from a traditional school or who had dropped out. There was

also a night school program at the site. Students did not have a formal graduation ceremony. They simply completed their credits and moved on with their lives. I had attended a "Robing Ceremony" at one of the local high schools; an advanced studies school in fact. This Robing Ceremony was a very emotional experience where students were able to acknowledge someone who had helped them along the way. These students, at the alternative school, had amazing stories they were able to tell during the ceremony. Of all the things accomplished at this school, the Robing Ceremony was a tradition that I was most proud of helping to start.

After considering the school's customs and traditions, think about the role you would like to play in these activities. Thoroughly examining your role in these activities is a great opportunity to strengthen the relationship that is developing between you, the staff, and the community at large. Students get a big kick out of silly or fun activities like throwing pies at the principal or putting her in a dunk tank. These are just a few of the extras that schools enjoy. Be careful about what you have promised. Make sure it's doable, affordable, and would look appropriate on television or on social media.

Now that you've examined and analyzed your school in general, let's look at more details. See table 1.1

Table 1.1. Dimensions of School

Dimension	Elementary	Middle	High
Staff	Number of core classes or compartmentalized classes option	Number of core classes	Number of required courses for graduation / auxiliary credits / department heads / senior sponsors / underclass sponsors
Schedule	Number of auxiliary classes (art, music, PE, STEM—for planning time)	Number of auxiliary classes (art, music, PE, STEM—for planning time)	Teacher or counseling committee in charge of master schedule
Library	Scheduled, open, or combination	Scheduled, open, or combination	Policies / services / community access
Parent/community	President / parent bulletin / marquee	President / parent bulletin / marquee	President / parent bulletin / marquee / showcases / booster
Security	Who / how many / procedures	Who / how many / procedures	Who / how many / procedures
Counseling	District counselors / procedure for outside counselors	District counselors / procedure for outside counselors	District counselors / procedure for outside counselors / student counseling policies and schedule change procedures / 100% student coverage plan
Special services	How many students / cases / meeting times	How many students / cases / meeting times	Case management / transitions
Communication	Webmaster / parent bulletin / marquee	Webmaster / parent bulletin / marquee	Webmaster / parent bulletin / marquee
Teacher organization	Union representative / meeting times	Union representative / meeting times	Union representative / meeting times

Dimension	Elementary	Middle	High
Special events	Pre-school meet the teacher / holidays / parent conference procedures / promotion	Pre-school meet the teacher / holidays / parent conference procedures / promotion / transition to high school	Prom / graduation / academic competitions / sports / special interests / pre-school freshman focus night
Duty schedules	Scheduling team	Scheduling team	Scheduling team / after-school-night duties
Health care	Immunizations verification / screenings / community services	Immunizations verification / screenings / community services	Immunization verification / screenings / community services
Transportation	Bus / car / walk procedures	Bus / car / walk procedures	Bus / car / walk procedures / student parking policies
Finance	School secretary or principal's assistant will track and monitor income and expenses	Financial secretary will track and monitor expenses and income	Financial secretary will track expenditures and income of the school and departments

Chapter Two

Know the Staff

- How large or small is the staff?
- How many and what kinds of departments are there?
- Are there deep divides within the staff?
- How invested in the school's success are the staff?
- Are the staff motivated by the same kinds of things, or highly individualized?
- Hiring new staff
- Retaining staff members
- What is alternative certification?

Starting the year on a positive note will determine future outcomes. Making a great first impression will set the stage for success, at least in the next few weeks. A good or at least neutral first impression helps everyone relax and focus on starting school. Take the time to get to know each and every staff member on an individual basis. Knowing staff members takes time and it won't happen after one or two "ice breakers" or team-building exercises.

Leaders can learn a lot about anyone if they take the time and listen carefully. First, seek to understand, and then seek to be understood. Listen and observe. On the other hand, be aware that leaders are also being noticed. The smallest, seemingly inconsequential action can be read in many ways by many people. So, consistency is a key aspect to being—or being perceived as—stable and reliable.

Personal Experience

At the small, rural school where I was first assigned as principal, I developed a severe image problem. Wanting to make a good impression as a smart, hardworking, and serious administrator, I still struggled with not being liked. In fact, a consultant was hired to help me figure out why this was happening. I had been successful at the largest elementary school in the district. After staff interviews, the consultant said that teachers throughout the building thought they were "in trouble." Why? The report said because I would march around the halls at a quick pace, looking mad. I had a serious case of "resting mad face." I had a walking style that said, at least to me, I am serious. I will quickly address problems and solve them. I have an eye on all for the good of all. Well, all of this was interpreted by my staff as "I don't trust you and I've got my eye on all of you incompetent people."

I had developed this manner of walking because my experience prior to this assignment had been at a building comprising three hundred thousand square feet, with three stories and a basement. There were nearly eight hundred students and forty-two teachers. The consultant advised me to slow my pace—"throw a brick in your wagon"—and literally paste a smile on my face whenever I was in the hall or other public space. I drew a wagon, cut it out and taped it by my door, along with a happy face next to it. The visual analogy helped me to see myself, not as I saw me, but as others did. This little reminder helped me to reflect on the impact I had on others. It helped me to see the fragile nature of relationships and how things could be interpreted by others much differently than I saw them.

As "boss," when you notice things are going downhill, you have to be brave enough to ask what's wrong and face the answer. I was afraid of getting the answer, then not knowing what to do about it. Definitely a learning experience for me.

Effective leaders are aware of their impact on others. How leaders walk, talk, and pace their conversations has an impact on how they are perceived. Get to know the staff and allow them to know you. No matter the size of the staff, a participatory management style works best among educators. An old saying goes, "People will go without having their way, but they won't go without having their say." Further, Stein and Book offer the view that "people resent being told what to do and certainly do not appreciate being ignored. Successful leaders today focus on winning the hearts and minds of the people around them. Without getting buy-in for their ideas, plans and tactics, there's little incentive for those around them to perform optimally. People want to be involved in the plans and their implementation. As well, they have to feel they have contributed. After all, if people feel they have some ownership of the initiative, they are more likely to want to see it succeed" (Stein and Book 2011, 270–71).

Schools are getting larger, some with thousands of students and a staff numbering in the hundreds. How can you get to know every staff member before school is over for the year? Building a strong group of educators requires a herculean effort to be involved in as many departmental meetings as possible. However, you certainly do not want to be in all meetings—your mere presence could signal your distrust in the department, the chairperson, or both.

Attend the meeting just enough so the members know you care and are truly focused on academic success. Be as positive as possible. Listen and learn. Ask questions and show encouragement. If the only time staff members see the principal is in a whole-school staff meeting, the staff is forced to rely on surface impressions to form conclusions about the principal, and they will perform based on those conclusions, good or bad. Worse still, if the only time an administrator talks to or is in classrooms is during evaluation, that makes it impossible for the teacher to accept honest feedback from you. Try to implement a form of team observation/evaluation. Be very careful and train teachers appropriately, using a mild, low-stakes format (see teacher evaluation form on publisher's website).

HOW LARGE OR SMALL IS THE STAFF?

Hopefully, you gained some knowledge about your school before you accepted your assignment. A few clicks on your laptop or phone and you have the basic information about the school situation to which you are assigned. That is, of course, the easy part. A principal's behavior and mode of operating is totally different if your staff is large versus if it is tiny. A small staff (one or two teachers per grade level or subject) usually finds itself behaving as a family. News travels quickly and without a principal's control or consent. Should the principal behave like a parent, or an older sibling? Do teachers report on one another? Bring every complaint to your door? Or does everyone operate in their own kingdom, barely speaking to each other? It depends on the dynamics already in place.

The administrator can usually find this out by observing the types of questions that are asked by the staff. This observation can only be done and will only be precise after working with the staff for a few weeks or months. Teachers may ask questions just to feel you out and not because they need actual information. Your answers will give the staff more information about you than about the content of the question. Answering queries outright and with certainty may give the impression that you know it all and are not willing to compromise. Answering with a question demonstrates your willingness to learn and be a part of the school team. Answer with questions like "How has this been done in the past?" or "How is this type of situation usually handled?" After all, problems didn't arrive with you; someone handled it before you came.

Finding out where you fit, within this family is key to your success as a principal. This is not to say that you do as you are told, and remain in this position of being new on the block with no ideas or insight. Behaving in a way that is more open will put your staff at ease so that your actions and suggestions are not immediately viewed as hostile but are seen in a more neutral way so that the channels of communication remain open. As you begin to take on your role in the family and inspire confidence, people will be more open to your ideas.

In a school with a large staff, the opportunity for everyone to get to know you is somewhat reduced. As in any big city, corporation, or other large organization, teachers don't expect to get to know you personally, and may expect change to be rapid or radical. Wise principals will spend most of their energy inspiring small groups of people within the total school community.

Your teams will be the people who will carry out the mission of the school. Spending time with your key teams (administrative, academic, athletic, auxiliary) will get you where you need to be. These relationships are vital to develop a healthy school environment. Building relationships with fellow employees is in many ways like being a good coach.

In the book, *Trillion Dollar Coach: The Leadership Playbook of Silicon Valley's Bill Campbell* (Schmidt, Rosenberg, and Eagle 2019) the authors say that to be a great manager, you have to be a great coach. Your success depends on helping other people to be successful. The book highlights how peer relationships are developed.

> As we noted earlier, Bill highly valued peer relationships. An important, often overlooked, aspect of team building is developing relationships within the team. This can happen organically, but it is important enough that it should not be left to chance. So Bill looked for any opportunity to pair people up. Take a couple of people who don't usually work together, assign them a task, project, or decision, and let them work on it on their own. This develops trust between the two people, usually regardless of the nature of the work.

This was during an individual relationship. Advice on coaching in meetings talks about making people feel a part of a team. "People would look forward to the meeting with Bill, because when Campbell ran a meeting or brought a group together, the environment was results oriented, everyone participated and contributed, and they actually enjoyed the meeting. It was positive and fun to be part of a team" (123).

Coaching before hiring:

> Pick the right players. The top characteristics to look for are smarts and hearts: the ability to learn fast, a willingness to work hard, integrity, grit, empathy, and a team-first attitude. (Schmidt et al. 2019)

Coaching on the job:

> Excellent teams at Google had psychological safety (people knew that if they took risks, their manager would have their back). The teams had clear goals, each role was meaningful, and members were reliable and confident that the team's mission would make a difference. You'll see that Bill was a master at establishing those conditions: he went to extraordinary lengths to build safety, clarity, meaning, dependability, and impact into each team he coached. (Schmidt et al. 2019)

Remind yourself of your role as a coach to build success into others. It is not just about you and your success.

Open and honest communication will inspire open and honest feedback. You cannot "win the war" if secrets are allowed to develop and fester. Will you be aware of all secrets?

Certainly not, and you would not want to know everything. You are not a god. If you establish yourself as one to be trusted, secrets that affect student or staff well-being are much more likely to be revealed than hidden.

Can the leader have a coaching relationship with students? Yes, but it will have to remain at somewhat of a distance for most students. Of course, there will be special situations where you get to know some students and their families, but mostly you have to remain in the role of the friendly lady at the top or the man who sometimes visits or comes to the cafeteria to say hello. It depends on the size of the school and how you are perceived. Allow your staff to do their jobs.

Alan Cutler in his book *Leadership Psychology* (2014), says, "To be an inspirational leader, you must understand your people: how they think: what they expect, and what they need in order to contribute to your vision. Leadership is all about recognizing the mutual dependency that exists between leader and follower. The relationship is symbiotic, with both parties requiring the support of the other if they are to grow and develop—even in some cases...to sustain life in extreme conditions" (259).

What will you do if everyone is doing his or her job? You will be enjoying your job. You will be busy developing your teams. Meetings will take up most of your time. Productive meetings are a powerful way to develop your relationship with your teams. Teams want to be seen, heard, and honored—not with trophies or certificates, but with your full attention. Give positive feedback, take their concerns seriously, and celebrate together.

In team meetings, ask someone to keep notes so that you can briefly review your progress at each meeting. Start with a brief review of prior meetings, but don't spend time rehashing past information. Take time to clarify, but try not to open old disagreements. Keep it current. Schools are about what's going on "now." Keep the focus on student impact. Continue to ask, "How does this impact students?" when the discussion strays into personal disagreements. Ask, "Is there a way we can work this out?" Your job is not to parent people, but to have them work out their own solutions.

It will be rare when you have to decide and declare. Both parties should ask for your guidance. Stepping into the role of parent will harm your relationship with people. You will be blamed for negative outcomes. Allow adults to be adults.

HOW MANY AND WHAT KINDS OF DEPARTMENTS (TEAMS) ARE THERE?

Principal's goals for teams: Teams functioning to their highest degree with no infighting. Teams staying in their lane and communicating with other teams so that toes are not stepped on or the work becomes dysfunctional such as in the scheduling of activities.

The most obvious type of teams are academic teams (e.g., math teachers). Second are student achievement teams (a variety of teachers cross two subjects). Then there are other teams (e.g., prom committee, graduation team, athletic teams of coaches). Should you, as leader participate in each team? Trust your team to do its job.

Most teachers want to avoid the principal becoming too involved in their teams and try to take care of their own business. That's when you need department heads to let you know if there are issues that cannot be handled at the team level, for example, authorizing expenditures. There is a saying, borrowed from the military: "Follow the chain of command." It sounds a little harsh and not at all collaborative, but it will really reduce confusion and virtually eliminate double actions. Let team members and colleagues know whom they are responsible to; whom to communicate with, and how procedures are done. If you explain why we have "chain of command," people will understand and do their best to comply.

In a large high school, the principal's task is, to a large degree, to train and employ staff members to "stay out of the news." This involves forming and *in*forming your team to ensure that the school is functioning on a legal, academically sound basis. Share good news early and often.

Your security team is a special team that you will need to have open, honest, and frequent communication with. Clear expectations regarding security must be established and maintained. We have seen the disastrous effect that a malfunctioning security team can have on the school and its students. Be proactive to avoid possible problems.

ARE THERE DEEP DIVIDES OR FACTIONS WITHIN THE STAFF?

"A house divided against itself cannot stand." Serious divides and factions will not work in any school. A principal can best handle these issues with humanity and humor. Find something that will break up these divides and

Table 2.1.

Team and Frequency of Meeting	Members	Purpose
Academic (horizontal) Quarterly	Core subject teachers of same grade level	Monitor academic achievement using test score data; insure equity
Academic (vertical) Quarterly	Core subject teachers across different grade levels	Monitor academic achievement using test score data; insure equity
Athletic Beginning and end of season	Sports coaches	Monitor athletic programs using win/loss data; expand programs; insure equity
Counseling Mid-year	Counselors and social workers	Monitor and advise students and their families on academic and psychosocial matters
Special education Mid-year	Special education teachers	Ensure compliance with federal law, train teachers on compliance, methods, and various ways to serve mainstreamed students
Security Weekly or as needed	Inside and outside security or police	Monitor safety inside and outside school area, plan and implement plan to maintain school safety.
Administrative As needed, minimum weekly	Principals	Monitor all aspects of student achievement, staff performance and building maintenance
Arts Mid-year	Visual and performing arts, physical education, ROTC, other auxiliary subjects	Ensure equal access to programs, heighten the school's profile in the community, enrich student options

encourage people to get to know each other around a non-issue, like college ball team loyalty, or dessert cookie favorites. Ignoring the issue won't help to resolve it, but open and honest communication will allow both parties to recognize and acknowledge that you know what's going on and are not pleased with it.

HOW INVESTED IN THE SCHOOL'S SUCCESS ARE THE STAFF?

How can you determine which of the staff members are invested in the success of the school? It is easy to see based on their actions, along with what they express verbally. Most of the time, people who have been employed at a school site for a long period are invested in its success, although not always. People who live in the area, whose children attended the school are usually highly invested. Employees who have seen principals come and go and who have ideas about each and every one of them, including you, may or may not be truly invested, but are simply watching the show.

How can you tell who is not invested and just working to get the needed experience and move on at the earliest opportunity? Some employees start the year with their own agenda, but develop an investment as time goes on.

Jeff Jones, in his book *Management Skills in Schools: A Resource for School Leaders*, discusses team member development: "The skills required to be an effective team leader in schools are many and varied, but personal management skills lie at the heart of getting the best from those that make up the team" (2004, xi). Later he makes the point that there is a need

> for each of us as team leaders to understand the intimate relationship between knowing, understanding and developing ourselves and knowing, understanding and developing our team members. . . .The evidence from a great deal of the research into improving school effectiveness points to the fact that teachers need support, encouragement and recognition of their achievements if they are to become more effective. Good performance management sets out to achieve this. (140)

Why is investment important? Obviously, a principal cannot make or force someone to be invested in the school, but if you take time to think about it, it will help you to determine the employee's motivation and help you decide how you'll need to approach your relationship with that person. An employee with deep connections not only with the other school employees, but with the surrounding school community could be your best friend and ally—or not.

Those employees who are not as invested are not as concerned about the community or how anyone, except you, their boss, feels about their work. They are willing to do what you ask and will refer to you if asked about what is expected from them. These usually new staff members are not a part of any clique and need much encouragement from you. In a small school, they will look to you for guidance until they feel they can trust other staff members. In a large school setting, their team is their first line for information.

ARE THE STAFF MOTIVATED BY THE SAME KINDS OF THINGS, OR ARE THEY A HIGHLY INDIVIDUALIZED GROUP?

How diverse is the staff at your school? Even within diverse groups, there is much individualization when it comes to motivation. Some teachers will spend a lot of money out of their own pockets for their students, because it's not the student's fault that money is running low. Others will campaign, march, and lobby for funding but will not spend one dime from their pay, because it is the district's or state's responsibility. These are individual views of approaching funding, developed by a teacher's motivation, which is informed by personal experience. It's not the principal's job to micro-psychologize each teacher, but to recognize that people are motivated by different things.

Cutler examines motivational aspects of finding good employees and cites a study that "identified the five most critical mindsets for individuals to feel engaged in any type of work" (Cutler 2014, 229). They are: optimism, a general positive outlook resulting in enjoying the job more; purposefulness, a calling, not just a job (Why am I here? Why am I doing this job?); autonomy, the extent of self-control one has over the task, real or perceived; competence, the ability to do the work at a high skill level (knowing how and when); and resilience, the ability to react positively and constructively when faced with adversity.

HIRING NEW STAFF

One of the most exciting aspects of being a principal is that of hiring new staff members. In all the excitement, there are serious challenges to be met. Some school districts are in the enviable position of having their choice of new graduates or experienced people looking for a change. Others struggle to fill open positions with competent candidates. Depending on the district, there may be a set of pre-determined questions that all candidates are expected to answer. This is an attempt to reduce bias in hiring. It is recommended that the team approach be taken when it comes to hiring or a combination of principal pre-screening candidates and then members of the department "chiming in" with their preferred selections.

Teacher teams may not always get their choice, but it is always nice "to be asked." Exercise extreme caution when explaining "why" someone was or was not hired. Legalities (ask the HR department or the district's legal team) are the main focus when answering any "why." It is best to stay with general statements such as "because they were the best qualified for our school." Keep your personal opinions out of it. There is too much room for misinterpretation of opinions to be aired. Resentment is the last thing you want when you were only seeking input to inform your final decision.

Personal Experience

We were seeking a person to take on the position of teacher for a highly challenging group of students. A person answered our posting. The person lived out of town, so we decided to interview them over internet viewing technology. It was noted that there was significant medical equipment in the background and that the candidate was seated in a wheelchair. In considering the ADA rules and the fact that we were in fact "desperate" to fill the position, we hastily hired this person. The person, after much effort and training, ended up attempting to sue the district, not on ADA grounds, but because of being truly unable, or unwilling, to fulfill the basic requirements of the job. After many days of absence and reasons why the person couldn't perform, we had to let the person go. We felt scammed by someone trying to make a living off the district. A year after this person was fired, I was still getting phone calls from our attorneys.

Even with the best of intentions, sometimes hiring mistakes occur. The one thing that will increase your chances of making a good hiring decision is to faithfully call and check references. It is very difficult, at times, to wait for the right person, but it is surely worth it.

RETAINING GOOD STAFF

People are happiest and most motivated when they feel they are fully utilizing their inherent or learned strengths. Leaders should, therefore, be continually aware of high-level capabilities that may, or may not be evident in employees' current job responsibilities. Once identified, it is the leader's obligation to ensure that employees are given the opportunity to fully employ their strengths for the benefit of the organization.

Does everyone want to be involved in leadership? Some teachers are willing and able. Through their experiences they have identified areas that need improvement and have definite ideas about how to proceed. This is where distributed leadership can be most effective. Train teachers in the particular aspects of these areas and allow them to lead. A principal can also enlist teachers into leadership by promoting small group leadership. Identify, or let teacher teams identify whom they want to lead their particular group. Alternating leaders is an efficient way to have a fully trained and capable staff.

Athletics motivates some people, academic achievement and scholarships motivates others. If the football team motivates large groups of people, wouldn't it make sense to get on the bandwagon and allow football to motivate the staff? Knowing a staff member has to pick up her children no more than one hour after school helps you to understand why she looks antsy in your staff meeting.

Also, recognize that motivations change. A major life event can cause motivation to shift so that the staff member you thought you knew so well is almost unrecognizable. Use whatever you can to help your staff feel respected and honored for the job they are doing. Thoughtfully spending time considering your staff's needs will help to reduce your problems and increase your success at school.

WHAT IS ALTERNATIVE CERTIFICATION?

Are good teachers made or are they born? Before there were colleges to train teachers, there were teachers. People whose simple love of learning and of teaching gathered students and taught them in homes and in schools. These people many times had very little in the way of materials and books, sometimes making up their own curriculum and using primitive reading and writing tools. Then we "evolved" to today, where a four-year degree complete with a few months of student teaching is required from most State Departments of Education. A fee is paid, a background check is completed and you are handed the keys to your classroom. Certainly, with all these credentials, at least you can be guaranteed a competent if not outstanding teacher!

Unfortunately, this has not worked out as intended. Today, many teachers have left the profession for more lucrative careers. And it is not only about money. Today's graduates are more than ever before willing to move to regions that have the lifestyle they prefer. Moreover, female students have many more career options than were had in the now distant past.

During this staffing crisis, many states have instituted a way for interested people to become teachers, much like the time before all the official certification requirements were instituted. All you need is a bachelor's degree in any subject (which demonstrates your ability to learn), and a willingness to be trained in educational psychology and methods (on the job, while you are teaching).

There is usually a committee whose responsibility is to guide you on your journey. The committee consists of a college professor, an administrator, and a fellow teacher. After having observed you in your classroom, this committee meets to discuss any areas you could improve on and to encourage you to keep trying. Some of the best teachers in America have come from this system of Alternate Certification. No matter where your teachers come from, each one should be valued for their skills, strengths, and willingness to learn. These new teachers rely on the coaching they receive from you, and more importantly, from their own team of teachers and day-to-day experiences with students and other colleagues.

Chapter Three

Informal Leaders

- Who are the most powerful or influential people in the building?
- Who are the most vocal people in the building?
- Are you willing to share power with them?
- What is the power source of this person?

As you begin your principalship, one of the most important concepts to consider and internalize is that the power seat does not always reside in the principal's office. In any group of people, there are natural leaders, natural followers, and some in between, depending on the topic or situation. You are the formal leader. You have been designated (not crowned) by the school district to lead your school to the top. There is a reason that you were chosen. Sometimes that reason will be revealed to you in a formal way. You will be told why you were hired and what your expectations are. Sometimes you will simply be handed the keys with a "Good luck."

That's formal leadership. Informal leadership is when someone, intentionally or unintentionally, seems to be attempting to run the school, take your place, control everyone, ruin your career, or a million other ways to say it. Study.com puts it this way: "Informal leadership is the ability of a person to influence the behavior of others by means other than formal authority conferred by the organization through its rules and procedures. Informal leadership is basically any type of leadership that is not based upon formal authority."

Leader Today says:

> An informal leader is someone within an organization or work unit who, by virtue of how he or she is perceived by his peers (or others in the organization) is seen as worthy of paying attention to, or following. The major thing that distinguishes an informal leader from a formal one is that the informal leader

does *not* hold a position of power or formal authority over those that choose to follow him or her.

The ability for an informal leader to influence or lead others rests on the ability of that person to evoke respect, confidence, and trust in others, and it is not uncommon for an informal leader to *not* intentionally try to lead.

Informal leaders can be exceedingly valuable to organizations, and to the success of formal leaders, *or*, if informal leaders do not support the formal leaders and their agendas and vision, they can function as barriers in the organization. (LeaderToday.org n.d)

There are people on the staff who may have wanted the position known as principal and, although the position is filled, still campaign for it. The person(s) who may have wanted the position holds court in the lounge or in parking lot meetings. In addition, these meetings are ongoing through texts, messaging apps, or calls. Parking Lot meetings are usually held immediately after the official staff meeting, and its agenda can be brutal. What is being said about you and your proposals or programs behind your back?

Most teachers simply want to teach their classes, have positive relationships with others, and go home to pursue other interests. Unfortunately, there are a few employees who, for whatever reason, want to be the leader, behave as if they are the leader, or find a way to inhibit the leader's goals. That will happen with almost any group. How do you get around it and minimize the extent of the distraction?

Effective leaders allow every person an opportunity to have their opinion heard in as constructive a way as possible. They make room for all opinions to be heard and give people an outlet to express their feelings and ideas about the subject at hand. Shutting down conversation and squashing opposing opinions forces people to find an outlet and a willing audience for them. How do you inject new ideas? Avoid making major decisions, even if everyone seems to be on board, after only one meeting. Nodding heads simply means that the people understand what you are saying and are being polite. It is a placeholder until people can take time to think about what you just said.

Principals usually know well in advance, usually weeks or months, what must be done, what decisions have to be made, and they have an outline and a time line already conceptualized, in their own mind. Communicate, communicate, communicate. Staff members are busy too and have their own agenda, pressings tasks, and concerns. Use all techniques to encourage people to think about what you are thinking about—conversations, emails, memos. Learning style theory isn't only for students.

Everyone has a preferred method of receiving and processing information. Visual learners like letters, memos, posted information, written information, complete with FAQs. Auditory people prefer to talk at length about the topic, express their opinions with you or in groups. Kinesthetic learners would like to make a visual representation of the concept using art materials or through role play. Using these methods can bring life to your staff meetings. "Sit and get" doesn't work very well with most topics, especially when it comes to getting new knowledge or processing new ideas. Your responsibility is to reach all stakeholders. Unfortunately, this is why staff meetings can be very lengthy. If time allows, break the subject into several meetings over time. Try for efficiency, but realize that to reach all, you'll have to employ at least two communication styles.

Francis discusses communication in *Principals' Personnel Characteristic Skills*:

> The principal needs to maintain cordial [interactions] and allow [the] free flow [of] information through the teacher to him/her. The principal needs to make the teachers feel [a] part of the school not as [a] visitor by giving full attention to their opinions and show affection to them always. A Principal that gives room for interaction with teachers by allowing teachers to approach him/her at [a] necessary time might result [in] high performance of teachers. (Francis 2019, 81)

The informal leaders on the staff are valuable team members. Some people are just naturally good with other people. They have a knack for getting all the information and knowing what is really going on in the school. If the formal leader is an introvert, he or she will need to seek out the extroverted teachers or informal leaders and make a special effort to become friends with them. It works in the reverse as well. The persons who are "opposite" of the leader mean no harm, but alienating them will be counterproductive to the leader and will inhibit success. All teams need "naysayers." These members can help discover holes in the leader's plans or help the leader to reach out to staff members who don't feel comfortable expressing their thoughts in an open meeting.

Robert Bacal of Leader Today defines informal Leadership in this way: "Informal leaders have some capabilities that more formal leaders do not, simply because they do *not* hold a position of designated authority. They can say things, for example, to other team members that could not be said by a person in an official management role, and their ability to influence is slightly different, since informal leaders are often perceived differently than formal leaders" (Bacal n.d.).

WHO ARE THE MOST POWERFUL PEOPLE IN THE BUILDING?

The sooner the principal can identify this person or this group of employees, the better for the working of the school. If you don't have a reliable source of information, you'll have to wait until you have gathered enough information through direct observation or other sources, such as the teacher's union representative. Many times, in a union school, the official union representative is powerful, and teachers look to him or her for guidance. This may be because people may have felt threatened by a prior administration and found themselves in a defensive position.

You will have to find ways to gently "disarm" the staff, make them feel comfortable and secure in knowing that you are here to protect and work with them as colleagues. This takes time. To increase your chances of success, try reaching out to teacher leaders before introducing the change initiative. Allow the "grapevine" to work to your advantage.

What do you do when the informal leader does not support your idea? One effective approach is to try to raise their level of knowledge about the proposed change. Have a series of discussions about what you are thinking to allow your colleagues time to think about it. Your goal is to get as much buy-in as possible. If you charge ahead, blindsiding everyone, especially the informal leader, without discussion, the chance of your instituting the change has decreased substantially. Allow your ego to rest. The point is not being the one with the answers, but getting consensus through discussion with others.

Don't give up at the first sign of resistance. Continue to work with the teacher leaders. You may not be able to sell your plan "as is" but working together, your team can help to modify the plan and perhaps take small steps in the direction of change. Yes, it takes more time to do it this way, but if your ideas or solutions are truly best, they will win. The idea will be instituted and the change made. Who cares about who thought of it? You may get the credit as principal of the school in the long run.

WHO ARE THE MOST VOCAL PEOPLE IN THE BUILDING?

Usually, the person who is most vocal in meetings expresses the unsaid thoughts of others on staff. Many times, this person simply has a personal need to be heard and recognized, but in the end, the rest of the staff may simply tolerate him and grant him no power or influence. He is known as always just being negative. If, on the other hand, the most vocal person is also the most influential, you must place him or her at top priority for developing a positive relationship. This doesn't seem fair to you or to the team, but if your teachers have granted this person power, there's not much you can do about it without causing people to take sides or inspiring open rebellion. Avoid meeting with this person one on one. You'll want to have a third, or fourth party involved. Until trust is built (and trust building goes both ways), group settings are usually a good idea. You don't want to be overprotective of yourself though; the aim here is to have open, honest communication for the benefit of all staff members, not just the vocal ones.

ARE YOU WILLING TO SHARE POWER WITH THIS COLLEAGUE?

What are the advantages to sharing power with a colleague? Won't this cause confusion among the staff members, within teams? How do you share yet maintain the proper balance with your being in charge? You are not abdicating your throne of power at school, you are reducing anxiety of staff, by letting everyone know that you are comfortable with shared leadership. You are redirecting attention and energy to the tremendous workload.

Lastly, but most importantly, you are helping others to recognize that they are a valued part of the team through your example. The main thing is to avoid this person being the only one with whom you share leadership. After all, they have their paid and assigned job to do as well. If they are spending half their time in your office with you, how is their job getting done? Is there a compromise between sharing and hoarding power?

This sharing of power works toward Jack Bagwell's model of distributed leadership:

> Additionally, principal leadership demands the skill of knowing how to motivate and empower others to address the social and academic needs of 99 diverse students. Since principals cannot undertake the task of school improvement as lone practitioners, they must seek out and enact alternative ways of engaging others in this work. A distributed leadership perspective offers a way for researchers and practitioners to examine leadership practice through the perspective of multiple individuals at all levels of the school, and to rethink how human capital can support school efforts to close the opportunity gap. (Bagwell 2019)

Worst case scenario: you resent or dislike the informal leader (justified or not). You refuse to give any power whatsoever to her. Like her or not, her power with staff members remains. She will use her power to undermine just about every initiative or action "of yours" that she wants. Staff members will see or hear about this war and will spend their valuable time trying to navigate the dynamics between the two of you. Now, where is your school? Is this the most positive situation? Use your emotional intelligence, remain calm, and work it out. There is too much at stake to keep this feud alive.

WHAT IS THE POWER SOURCE OF THIS PERSON?

Where does this person get their power? Is he the only teacher who knows how the computer systems work and is closely guarding the secrets? Is he so charismatic that everyone is under his spell? Is this group closely tied to a source of major funding? If you can determine where the power comes from, you'll have to decide if it is worth attempting to dethrone people like this rather than working with them. You can try to outperform such people and learn everything they already know, or try to widen your network to get your own sources of revenue, but why? There are other ways to spend your time besides trying to snatch informal power from a colleague.

After identifying any informal leaders, examining their power and its source, you still remain in the position of having to share power with them. Even if this sharing is not acknowledged, no meetings are held, and you decide to ignore them and move on, you still will be sharing power. Your best strategy is still to remain positive in all your interactions with all staff. Allow people to work in their own "wheelhouses," be grateful that you have such wonderful, skilled, and accomplished personnel and move on for the good of the school.

Chapter Four

Know the Community

- What kind of environment is the school located in?
- Are there recent changes that have had a major impact on the school?
- What is the psycho/social makeup of the school community?
- What are consistent issues that must be dealt with?
- Who are the community leaders?
- What type of communication is preferred by the community?

Principals work in schools located in all types of communities. Principals in schools located in struggling neighborhoods may have unique, difficult, or intractable problems and situations to deal with. Schools with an abundance of resources and highly involved parents and staff can be home to struggling principals too. The struggles of a leader are sometimes masked by the abundance of resources. In either case, correctly identifying or "reading" the community is necessary for success as principal. "The role of the principalship, especially in hard to staff schools, is constantly being redefined by today's changing social and educational landscape. The vision of tomorrow's school leader is an archetype that is more community leader than CEO" (Stafford and Hill-Jackson 2016, 76).

Some principals' entire career is spent in struggling inner-city schools. How were these leaders effective? How did they find the key(s) to success? First these principals had a positive view of their situation. They did not allow the press or what has been said about the school or its community to determine how they felt about its students and their families. The principals have an attitude of determination. They know that every child can succeed despite their circumstances.

What about money and other resources? Every community has resources. Parents in poor communities are not disengaged. The parents are busy. Busy working two or three jobs. Busy caring for children. Yes, sometimes they are otherwise engaged with activities such as drug use. But so are people in affluent communities. A struggling school may not have a big parent organization or generous and consistent donors, but it doesn't mean people don't care. Your job is to keep the community informed and invited to come in. The coming in may not be a physical or actual coming into the school, but participation in sales, elections, and so on. Try to figure out what works for your school's relationship with the community.

The school's marquee may be the only news that parents will read. Communication is about taking time to talk to parents when they come in, listening to people when they call, and making sure they feel they are being heard. The district report can wait until after school hours. The nature of the job of principal is people, not reports. Find a way to delegate reports to other members of your team.

The perception of the school community depends on their perception of how the principal spends his or her time. The community doesn't care how many reports you filed on time. They only care about their children being safe and adequately educated. The community's perception of you is largely in your control. At the elementary school level, especially, the community likes to see the principal. In that case, high visibility is demanded. Middle and high school parents demand a principal who is diligent in responding to problems. Don't become a victim to the vicious cycle of bad community relations—they don't like me, so why should I care?—which makes their perception of you even worse.

Here are some actions that will influence the way the community sees you:

1. Leaving before the last employee leaves. If you must leave, at least contact the late-staying teachers and see if they are OK, and ask if they need anything before leaving. The point is showing your genuine regard for others. It's like the saying about restaurants. People may not say how pleased they were, but will tell ten people if they were not. With school staff, people will let others know about how caring the principal is. "Do unto others as you would have them do unto you."
2. Bad-mouthing the school and its stakeholders. If you say or write "bad reviews" of your school or its employees, how is anyone else going to feel about your school?
3. Treating others unequally. Make every effort to treat coworkers in a fair manner. Remember that fair is not always equal. Avoid glaring discrepancies in treatment.

These are only a few. If you are not sure about how you are perceived, do some reading on image consulting, or how to improve your image. Observe others in the public view; note how they act and react to different situations. Note how you feel in your gut after having been in their presence. Like it or not, you are a public figure, not just another school employee.

The Intercultural Development Research Association (IDRA) defines appropriate community engagement: "Authentic family and community engagement is personally, culturally and linguistically appropriate, consistent, persistent, and ongoing. It is an invitation to speak and be listened to, and is reflected in critical conversations" (Intercultural Development Research Association 2019, 5).

For school districts, providing opportunities to engage the broader community and hearing multiple perspectives can serve to improve policy and practice. Methods for engaging the community may include conducting periodic community and parent surveys as well as focus groups with participants across the district about perceptions around diversity.

Your local police and fire departments are usually willing to attend the occasional parent night. If your school is a true community school, counseling and health organizations are already a part of the environment and can also attend parent events.

Developing or maintaining positive school culture is an essential aspect of school improvement efforts that can lead to increased student engagement and achievement. A positive school culture plan employs techniques to engage stakeholders in shared responsibility for implementing educationally sound practices.

IDRA also states, "Community engagement (including community and faith-based organizations, local businesses, housing complexes) is critical to the support of academic achievement and transformational change. To engage communities and families more effectively, schools must ensure that programs match the needs and shared interests of the families and communities that they serve. Schools may begin by actively reaching out to communities and mapping the assets they bring" (Intercultural Development Research Association 2019, 13).

IN WHAT KIND OF ENVIRONMENT IS THE SCHOOL LOCATED?

While thinking about your school, how would you describe the neighborhood that surrounds it? Is the school located in a large city within the downtown area, or is it in a rural country atmosphere? Are the children bused in to the site, or do most walk? Most schools receive a mix of car riders, walkers, and bus riders. Their mode of transportation is only one way in which to describe and think about the community. Are the families a heterogeneous mix with many students in constant transition or a homogenous group of families where most of the children have been in school together for a number of years? Demographic descriptions will influence many things from the mundane (classroom assignments, master scheduling) to the extraordinary such as disputes and how various situations are handled. For example, keeping children of feuding families out of the same classroom or policies, for example, on separating twins.

ARE THERE RECENT CHANGES THAT HAVE HAD A MAJOR IMPACT ON THE SCHOOL?

Has the school district undergone sweeping changes that require the administration to spend extra time building new teams of teachers? Revamping student expectations or changing long-standing traditions can take a toll on the amount of time available for instruction. Some schools have had to physically move to another building and integrate with an existing school due to massive reconstruction or remodeling needs. Physical changes, such as moving, require a lot of work, but the psychological challenges that occur when students and teachers are remixed and blended require a much different set of skills and usually, more time.

WHAT IS THE PSYCHO/SOCIAL MAKEUP OF THE SCHOOL COMMUNITY?

A community is more than buildings, streets, and people. What are the people like within the community? Are parents angry because of past misconduct of staff or failed policies? Is the neighborhood undergoing change from gentrification or from neglect? Are parents materialistic? Is the atmosphere competitive and cliquish? Is the school a steady and consistent force in the neighborhood? These questions are worth considering before starting, or within the first few months of school.

Personal Experience
Even when you have the best intentions, there will be people who will dislike or distrust you. It was at the end of a busy yet productive day. A student had gotten into some trouble that resulted in his being sent home. The student's parent was unavailable for a conference that day, so the much older brother was sent in to get clarification and to discuss the punishment. After a brief discussion of what the student had done and why the discipline was taken, the brother pulled out a cell phone and simply said, "Did you hear that?" God was with me that day, because I didn't react at all. I probably looked puzzled, he may have thought I would have lost it and begin to berate him, but I didn't. I credit God and the experiences I have had over the past twenty or so years in education. I won't forget that day.

WHAT ARE THE CONSTANT ISSUES THAT MUST BE DEALT WITH?

Are there intractable issues that require you to spend an inordinate amount of time tracking and intervening? Issues such as low attendance, high truancy, fights, burglary/theft, staffing changes? If you are assigned to a school with issues such as these, unfortunately, you will have to take time from "normal" priorities and deal with them. Be sure to enlist others to complete the required forms that accompany such events.

    The best way is to first establish teams to focus on these issues. You will need to be in on the meetings to show that you are serious and that you expect real change. Next, you will need to encourage staff to remain positive and focused on academics. Do not publicize these meetings as ones that will "solve all our problems." Focus on getting information and allowing parents to sometimes vent their frustration. Keep public meetings focused on the good that is happening in your school. Keep school activities going on schedule. Most students and their parents are good people who mean well. All parents are concerned, but some may not know how to channel their energy for the good of their child. Don't let the few determine what your school is all about. Control the message as best you can. Establish a publicity committee and let them work for good.

WHO ARE THE COMMUNITY LEADERS?

In every group of people, including parents, there are informal leaders, people who exert influence on others. In a large community, you will probably know who these folks are. They will usually make themselves known and offer to help. In a smaller community, you may or may not know, right away, who they are. These people can be of help to you. Get to know them with an invitation to chat. Seek them out at school activities. Conversely, if they are simply a gossip, your efforts may not be fruitful at all. That's fine. You can't control what other people do. The only thing you can control is what you do. Continue to do good and let your actions speak for you.

WHAT TYPE OF COMMUNICATION IS PREFERRED BY THE COMMUNITY?

Although they are not school employees, you will need to communicate with the surrounding community. This one-way communication can always be misunderstood because you don't get immediate feedback to check for accuracy. Does your community value the written word? Then use the outdoor marquee. Do robo calls make your parents angry? Use them judiciously and only for emergencies or other vital information. Keep a running list of your calls (most software programs do this automatically). Do your parents spend time online? Decide which site you will use for your parents.

Meet with your team to decide which one you'll use. You don't want parents chasing down information for multiple children's classes via multiple applications. Do parents value and focus on what their child's teacher is asking? Classroom letters from each teacher are appropriate and usually expected. For consistency, determine, as a staff, how often classroom letters are distributed. Do parents look at the marquee and depend on it for major events? Does the community support the activities of the school? You can get the answers to these questions through polls and through observation. Count the number of community members or non-school persons who attend, for example, the winter program or any after-school event.

Remember, the community is in your school as much as your school is in the community.

Chapter Five

Know the Goals of the District and School

- What are the goals of the school district?
- What are the goals of the school?
- Is the community aware of these goals?
- Is the staff aware of the goals?
- Time-sensitive goals

Your day has gotten off to a wonderful start; everyone is in their place and things are humming along. The phone rings. It's a representative from one of the many departments "downtown" or at "central office." Where's my what report? Due when? How did I miss this? The purpose of this chapter is to alert the new principal about various items that he will be responsible for, coming from "outside" your school.

The principal's responsibilities include meeting goals. Your primary goal is to use resources to educate students. Besides the goals that you have developed on your own, principals are given goals. The powers that are above you (district, state departments) will ask for a written document outlining the school's goals. The leader's primary goal is to increase student achievement. At any school, at all levels, with all students, academic progress is expected. Even in the most academically advanced school, improvements are always on the radar. Maybe there are equity or gender gaps that must be addressed. As principal, you will have to prove that you are working toward this goal. Detailed written plans are required.

There is a significant amount of pressure on the principal to improve something that professionals have little control over. Yes, professionals control the academic factors that lead to high achievement. Academic performance is totally under the school's control. The more challenging part of increasing achievement is influencing the underlying factors that school professionals have no control over, such as students' home environment, parent or other adult influences, economic background, and many others. Improvement is demanded regardless. Principals must remain calm when efforts to improve student achievement seem to be disregarded or are not recognized in the face of great odds. There are times when you may feel as if your job is on the line.

Because reaching academic goals is such a major part of what you do, a lot is riding on the progress of the school. Everyone wants their school to be at or near the top. Parents, taxpayers, governmental officials, and real estate professionals all need schools to do well. It seems the entire economy needs good schools! Thus, meetings are held to discuss school progress. *Your* school's progress. With all the "eyes" on education, the principal's job is very stressful.

Turk and Wolfe highlight the stressors that educational leaders encounter daily:

> These stressors result from external and internal sources. Given the emphasis on increased accountability measures in public education, principals experience pressures from external sources, such as federal and state mandates. Additionally, local stakeholders often present additional challenges for principals. Furthermore, the increased emphasis on school safety has presented principals with further roles, responsibilities, and resulting stressors. These multiple external pressures present continually increasing challenges for principals in today's public education climate. (Turk and Wolfe 2019, 150)

There it is, on display for all to see, your school's data displayed in six-inch letters at the bottom of the chart. All the hard work and progress you and your staff have achieved is reduced to one or two numbers at the bottom of the list of schools. Try not to take it too personally, but it actually is personal. The principal is the instructional leader, although no one leader can impact student achievement by herself. Everyone knows this. Your supervisors understand this fact. But it is you whom they expect to lead the improvement mission and to provide an explanation of why you are at the bottom and on a plan for improvement.

Your job, then, is to figure out how to enlist the help of your team. The entire team is needed to improve the school's data. After all, each data point represents actual children. It represents their chance for a good life, a chance to fulfill wishes and dreams, possibly an escape from poverty, or simply to access better opportunities. Because this is such a herculean effort, enlisting the help of your team will increase the likelihood that these goals will be realized and that your students will improve.

When you bring your data back to your school team, realize that they have been with their classes, working hard in a different, nonadministrative world. Realize that their concerns are far from the downtown meeting concerns. Your job is to bridge what is happening in their classroom with what is expected by the entire community. Actually, the expectations are the same because the community includes teachers as well.

Although there will probably be teachers or other school staff members who do not live in your immediate community, they are still a part of the larger community, and by choosing a career in education, they do have a vested interest in good schools. Enlist your teams to develop specific goals for your students. Your biggest challenge will be to keep team goals in the minds of staff as you go through the year. Teachers tend to focus their efforts on the day-to-day interactions and instruction of students, so the overall school goals that they've spent hours developing fade into the background.

Try to keep a broad, long-term view when you consider goals. Data meetings can get heated, as people tend to blame others and feel defensive about their practices. If you can control your emotions and consider the emotional impact on others, it will help to keep everyone cool and calm. However, you must strike a balance between maintaining calm and managing the urgency of the situation. You don't want to be so calm that your staff mistakes it for a noncaring attitude, but also avoid getting so overworked that your emotions get out of control. To keep things in perspective, ask yourself, "Will this matter in ten years?" or "Who will it matter to?"

This sanity strategy sounds dismissive, but a dismissive attitude won't work either. The aim is to encourage and coach others so they may be successful, which will lead to successful students. It is a matter of keeping your perspective so that you won't become paralyzed or angry by obsessing about the goals. Goals are written so that a plan with specific steps can be followed, so that people can spend their time and effort *working*, not *worrying*. "Principaling" is different from teaching; both are accountable to others, but the "clientele" is different. Teachers owe students their maximum effort every day (supporting and coaching). Principals owe teachers their maximum effort every day (also supporting and coaching).

WHAT ARE THE GOALS OF THE SCHOOL DISTRICT?

School districts are compared with one another statewide. The state Department of Education is accountable to the tax-paying public. Those state departments are compared nationwide with the departments of education in other states. Your small part in this is to help raise your district's ranking, which impacts both state and nationwide rankings.

As with school rankings and goals, each district has separate departments that have goals with which you are expected to assist. Each of these departments will have its own state or federal guidelines that they must meet; hence their own goals. To help you organize district goals, see table 5.1, which is a list of district departments to which you will be responsible. Remember in undergraduate college, when you just knew that each professor believed that their class was the only class you had? Well, every department appears to believe that their goal is the only objective you have to meet. Yes, they may acknowledge that you are busy and apologize for disturbing you, but they really need x, y, and z. From you. Now. This chart will give you a preview of what could be expected from you and to help you organize or add items to your calendar. Unless you have a great memory, organization is required so that you can form (and inform) teams and work on these tasks together.

As early as possible in the year, make an attempt to touch base with all the department heads or their assistants to establish a positive or at least neutral tone for the upcoming year. These district departmental staff members also have a huge job, working with every school at every level. They too

Table 5.1. Goals Chart

Department	Purpose	Type of Report / Frequency
Special Services	Ensure compliance with federal regulations regarding students with special needs	Students on individual education plans / yearly team meeting for each student
Title I	Ensure compliance with federal regulations regarding students of poverty and programs served	Yearly, with monthly updates
Accreditation	Audit of programs, teaching staff, teaching assignments, other state-determined items	Yearly
Academic departments	Book / resources spending and/or adoption. special programs	Yearly
Human Resources	Hiring, firing, increased or reduced allocations for staff	As needed; usually once at the beginning of the year, then once in the spring, for the upcoming term
Your immediate supervisor	Checking in with you, usually if there is a problem; impromptu visits; special meetings as needed.	As needed; once in the spring for your evaluation. Monthly meeting with all administrative staff

want to succeed and are, frankly, sometimes intimidated by you or conversely, trying to intimidate you.

Should you have questions, first attempt to increase your knowledge about these departments. Read about existing laws and procedures, ask your colleagues or supervisor, then call with your questions. These departments are as busy as you are, but they are willing to help. They don't mind questions, just be sure to use your time (and theirs) wisely.

WHAT ARE THE GOALS OF THE SCHOOL AND HOW ARE THEY DEVELOPED?

At the beginning of each year, gather several teachers. Ask veteran teachers, because novice teachers are too focused on surviving their first year. Their plates are full. Provide each team member with recent or last year's data organized for their review. Depending on how much time you have before the students arrive, it's recommended that teachers filter through the data on their own. This helps teachers learn how data is put together and come to their own conclusions about improvement.

If, as is usually the case, time is short, have the data ready for teachers. How far should teachers drill down with data? If your school has a highly mobile population, a focus on individual students won't be as productive as keeping it on large groups, for example, third-grade math, fifth-grade reading. What are the weak areas? What is on the state test? Who are the bottom students? Who needs intensive intervention?

Track your goals and review quarterly progress. Make adjustments and discuss recommendations. Use SMART Goals (Specific Measurable Attainable Relevant Timely). You will also need to reserve time on your calendar for regular data meetings. These data and goal-tracking meetings will be a source of encouragement to teachers, as they will be able to see improvements in their students. Save your findings; you'll need to provide the same data sets for grants and other departments, and to share with people who have a stake in your school (parents, community).

In addition to academic goals and anything you want to track for improvement or for grant reporting, there are goals such as improving student behavior or increasing parent involvement. Is behavior a major element in the needs of the students? Is parent involvement needed? You can set goals for any need that is identified. If you don't count it, you can't improve it, at least not with intent. Remember to celebrate goal achievements. It needn't be a big party, sometimes just a verbal or written acknowledgment is best. People remember anything with food. Reward hard work, even if things aren't working out exactly as planned.

IS THE COMMUNITY AWARE OF THESE GOALS?

With all the goals setting, do parents or students even know there are goals for your school? Parents' interests go beyond school-wide academic achievement. Elementary parents are concerned about safety, that their children being accepted, and that they are passing or being challenged to their potential. High school parents care about safety, graduation, and college/job preparation. The community at large cares about the school's reputation; good schools are tied to property value. These are your tax payers, and they want to get their money's worth.

IS THE STAFF AWARE OF THESE GOALS?

Most teachers, unless they are on the "school improvement" committee, are unaware of goals. They may be concerned in only a superficial way. Teachers' goals may range from survival to beating the team average. Goals shift and change. A teacher with an aging parent or a sick child may go from being a superstar to being an employee who is barely surviving the semester.

TIME-SENSITIVE GOALS

All good goals come with a ticking clock. Improve (what) by (how much) by (insert deadline). Evaluations are another goal that can extinguish a good principal's relationships with teachers. Some of these systems are overly detailed and need many hours of training and follow-through in order to complete even one evaluation. Others are a simple checklist of twenty to thirty items with a space for comments. If you work in a district where the teacher's union is very powerful, that adds another dimension to completing evaluations.

Yearly evaluations are basically a Keep or Dismiss for staffing. They are not as useful as the informal coaching (continuous improvement) that is done on a daily basis. A new form of coaching, peer-to-peer, is an effective form of informal coaching. Evaluations are tricky because any suggestions can lead teachers to feel their job is threatened or that they are not meeting the standard or that they are personally disliked. Building the right relationships with people will help teachers to understand the principal's intent because they understand the principal.

Federal funding (usually Title I) plans are a time-sensitive goal, with many benchmarks to track between the beginning of the year and the end goal or end of the year. If you put them on your calendar, it will help you avoid being blindsided and have to pull people into meetings in a hurry—or worse, ask people to stay late, interrupting their already tight schedule.

Chapter Six

Know Yourself

- Who are you in your role as a principal?
- What kind of principal do you aspire to be?
- How different are you outside of school than you are inside or school?
- What is your motivation for being principal?
- What are your deal breakers?

Why is this chapter near the end of the book? Shouldn't we have begun with an examination of yourself? Why not start with the principal? Because it is not about any one person. Yes, you are the leader, but you are a part of a group. The organization is not focused on any one person, even the leader. The school body is what is important. However, people need to know themselves and how they fit into the group. So spend some time thinking about your own worldview and how it influences your day-to-day actions and interactions with people. This is not a one-time exercise; you must continue to do so throughout the year. Evaluate your own motives, keep checking your emotional IQ, and see if your actions are consistent and predictable.

This chapter will guide you through knowing yourself as a leader. It will give you perspective and provide you with specific tips that will help you see yourself more clearly. It will help you to see yourself as others see you. It will help you to discover blind spots and identify areas where you can change immediately, or begin the work for long-term change.

WHO ARE YOU IN YOUR ROLE AS A PRINCIPAL?

Having an idea of who you want to be is a good place to start. The problem is when administrators get stuck in their idea of who they are (or want to be), without considering the true reality of their view. Take a good hard look at yourself without filters or blinders. Team dynamics, along with the particular school situation may warrant a different type of leadership than you may have imagined for yourself. The role of the friendly guy who has a joke for every occasion, that person who served you well at your last school, may not fit with people who are used to or prefer a more structured, serious principal. Conversely, you may need to shed some of the stilted, overly organized personality if your staff or community are more relaxed or nontraditional. You'll need to spend some time analyzing what will work in the particular situation in which you find yourself.

At least, for the first year, you will need to fit in more or less where people expect you to fit in. Change is a slow process. Don't throw your staff into defensive panic by "taking over," behaving in a nontraditional way, or doing what your stakeholders believe to be non-traditional.

Emotional Intelligence

First, begin by assessing your Emotional Intelligence quotient. A basic definition of Emotional Intelligence is having empathy. Empathy helps you to really hear what other people are saying and feel what they are feeling. Leaders who have a finely tuned sense of empathy care about their community; about less fortunate people. So they tend to be more participatory in their leadership style.

Most people *feel* empathy, but the disconnect comes when they fail to *show* empathy. Principals may think that showing empathy will cause others to believe that he is showing favoritism or that she is weak.

Schmidt, in the book *Trillion Dollar Coach*, writes about "fairness and favors." He advises leaders to help people by being generous with their time, connections, and other resources.

> Helping people and being generous tie right back to the concepts of love and community. If your best friend asks you to do a favor, you do it, right? You love your friend, you trust her judgment (usually), you would do anything for her, so when she asks you to do something that would help her and it's the right thing to do, there's no hesitation. But if she's your colleague at work, suddenly it's not so easy . . . someone might somehow perceive that it's not fair, its. So you don't do the favor. It's okay to help people. Do favors. Apply judgment in making sure they are the right thing to do, and ensure that everyone will be better off as a result. Then do the favor. (Schmidt et al. 2019, 176)

How can you determine if your image of yourself is in line with most of your staff, parents, and community? A brave person will ask others how they are perceived and be willing to open their mind and heart to receive such sensitive thoughts from a trusted friend or colleague. Here are some elements of personality/image for your consideration.

- Body Language—There is much information regarding body language and nonverbal communication. Posture, changes in tone, or inconsistencies can be detected by others on an intuitive level or in a more obvious way, through your actions.
- Habits—We all have unconscious habits that can be detected by others: "She always drops by the lounge after morning opening." "He always addresses women as Ms. while men are addressed by their first name." The video camera is a powerful tool. Try placing one in your office and reviewing it when you're feeling strong and confident; avoid viewing it at the end of a bad day.
- Policies—Staff may realize that chewing gum is a no-no, but it doesn't bother the leader if participants send or receive text messages during a meeting. Are your policies consistent? Control your emotions to avoid making impromptu pronouncements that you may later regret.
- Branding—What is the overall image that you consistently project. This is your brand. There was a professional who always, without fail, wore a black pantsuit each and every day. Her hair was neatly done at all times and in the same style. She was immediately recognized as principal; she exuded confidence and respect; just from her appearance. Are you the athletic administrator? The rabble rouser? The woman of few words? The tech savvy person? Never underestimate the power of image.
- Leadership Style—Leadership style is your personal way of running your school, of doing business. Are you the autocratic "my way or the highway" type or the more participatory, democratic kind of leader? Do you believe you are democratic while your actions and reactions tell a different story? Find the time to do some reading on leadership styles, and be sure that your words and actions are consistent with what you believe.

WHAT KIND OF PRINCIPAL DO YOU ASPIRE TO BE?

Most people who enter the principalship have thought about what kind of principal they want to be. That's fine. The only problem with that is that it is still a self-centered point of view. Maybe you feel you want to be a "benevolent dictator." A kind and thoughtful person but one who expects everyone to do what you say. Immediately. Without question. Having an idea of who you want to be is a good start to knowing what your actual role will be. The problem is when administrators get stuck in their idea of who they are (or want to be) without considering who they *need* to be. Team dynamics and the school situation at large may warrant a different type of leadership than what you may have imagined for yourself.

When people look back on your principalship—*if* they look back—how will you be remembered? Don't kid yourself thinking that people will spend hours of their precious time remembering you fondly or cursing the day you were born because of something you did or didn't do. You may do this, but they won't. People are far too preoccupied with their own lives to worry about you. Putting your "legacy" into perspective requires thinking about how you conduct yourself on a daily basis. You basically want to disappear into your role. Not that you don't want to have an impact, because you certainly do.

Your overall goal is to be a tool for success, not the star of the show. Your aim is to structure the environment so that people can say, "That was a great school, and my child really did well there." Some principals feel they have to put on the cape and save the day, sometimes by any means necessary, so they set out to do battle. These administrators end up being the ones to lose. The forces of many against one person are far too strong. Even in the best of circumstances with ready, willing, and able staff, you cannot do it alone. So, getting in where you fit in is best for novice principals. Pick your battles and behave kindly. Give people time to build up their trust in you, no matter your reputation or experience level.

One tool you may use is a simple continuum of a very basic personality trait. The exercise goes like this, and has exactly one question: Are you a task-oriented person or are you a people-oriented person? Pick a number between 1 and 15.

           Task Oriented   People Oriented
       1 2 3 4 5 6 7 8 9 10 11 12 13 14 15

Find where you are, then think about the people on your teams, or the staff as a whole. You may want to use this tool to help the staff identify where they are as they interact with one another, and with you. This simple tool will help you have a light bulb moment to answer why there are issues, or better, why people get along so well.

Alan Cutler quotes Ann Francke, CEO of Chartered Management Institute: "Even ethics can be learnt in the sense that when you are made aware that you are being too task-focused at work and that you need to be more caring, you can access that part of yourself" (Cutler 2014, 108)

Personal Experience

One school term, during a budget crisis, my tiny school had closed. I was chosen to work with a principal who had great success with her inner-city school. She had been there for many years; many people identified her school as just that: "Mary's school." She was, of course, very friendly and was on great terms with her staff. We got along well, but were completely opposite personality wise. "Mary" scored a 15 (totally people oriented). I scored a 1 (totally task oriented). We found ourselves negotiating the division of labor and how we related to the staff, volunteers, and parents, all year long. Looking back, it was really odd how we so differently met each challenge. We remain friends, but at the time, it was a little rough. For everyone.

In Cutler's book *Leadership Psychology*, he quotes William Rogers: "It is not just sufficient to lead by example, albeit that is the most important factor, you also have to back that up with some hard-nosed investment in time and money that focuses on your middle management, so that they can push that culture further themselves" (Cutler 2014, 105).

What do most employees feel are the traits of a good leader? Here are a few from Cutler (2014, 108):

- Good communicators and listeners
- Energetic and enthusiastic
- Calm under pressure
- Self-confident
- Prepared to take personal responsibility for decisions
- Comfortable in other people's company
- Good team player
- Convincing and persuasive
- Adaptable
- Recognizes own strengths and weaknesses

Cutler goes on to point out: "For many who are taking a first step on their leadership ladder, or indeed those already holding executive positions, it can be a journey of self-discovery. Effective leadership development programmes will include opportunities for participants to examine their own characters, values, behaviours and motivations. . . . Understanding who you are as a leader will help you develop both yourself and those around you" (Cutler 2014, 109).

HOW DIFFERENT ARE YOU OUTSIDE OF SCHOOL THAN YOU ARE INSIDE OF SCHOOL?

It's been said that you can fool some of the people some of the time, but you can't fool all the people all the time. At this time in our history, social media makes certain that you can't fool anyone. Compartmentalizing your life will only work to a certain extent. You can't be an evening pole dancer or numbers runner and be a daytime principal. This is an extreme example, but the truth is, you have to pick a persona and be comfortable with it. Face the fact that principalship is a twenty-four-hour job.

If there is a school fire, you need to be there. When tragedies happen, it's your "face" that is seen. When you retire or leave the educational arena, you can (basically) do whatever you wish, with whomever you want. The smaller the community, the more this is true. People usually prefer the more traditional administrator. However, the public is sophisticated enough in their knowledge of school policy that they expect a level of competence so that their children can be productive and succeed. The public's standards of personal conduct are varied, so, overall, people are much more willing to identify and focus on the issues that work toward making the school successful in its function. You can be or do whatever you want, as long as your school does its job. Please be advised, though, that your job, your image, your brand as a principal, does not stop at four o'clock or at the school door. The principalship is a seven-days-a-week job.

WHAT IS YOUR MOTIVATION FOR BEING PRINCIPAL?

Why did you choose the principalship?

Personal Experience

I'll tell you a little secret. The principalship chose me. I never, ever had a desire to be a principal. In fact, I nicknamed myself, "The Accidental Principal." God had other plans for me. I needed to learn (a lot) about people, about relationships, and about myself. After many years of being in the classroom, a single parent with two growing children, I thought I would get an advanced degree, specializing in curriculum, because I love books, including textbooks, and teaching. I could further my career by advising schools about which were the best book series to purchase. Well, there were no degrees in "curriculum," only certificates in "School Administration." Close enough. When openings came around, there were also no openings in the Curriculum Department. I had a degree in school administration though. Surprise, I was interviewed and selected. The rest of the story is in this book and I hope it will help you to succeed and thrive in your role.

If your motivation is to be the boss, to tell everyone what to do (because you know best), how to do it (because you know best), and when, please stop reading now and consider a job in the nearest retail establishment, insurance company, or bank. Being the boss will work for some jobs, but it works for very few learning communities. Most teams that continue to grow and achieve ascribe to the shared (or distributed) leadership model. Distributed leadership has been proven to be one of the most, if not the most, effective ways to operate in a school environment. See table 6.1

Rehman and colleagues discuss additional leadership styles: instructional, transformational, and moral leadership:

> Arguably, the most recognized leadership styles in school contexts are instructional, transformational, and moral; however, all of these leadership styles have some pros and cons. The transformational leadership style has been criti-

Table 6.1.

Leadership Type	Characteristics	Result
Distributed	Motivated by the team Gets buy-in from others Focus on results, not blame or credit	Better-quality decisions because team members are closer to the problem
Autocratic	Motivated by being in charge Leader gets all the blame or credit	Mixed quality of decisions Leader is out on a limb because of isolation
Instructional	Leader perceived as authoritative and task focused Exceptionally high status of leader	Stakeholders develop low level of vested interest and high level of isolation Low status of "followers"
Transformational	Aimed at realizing radical change Leader empowers members of the school to improve from within Leader may be considered a hero	Stakeholder confusion due to perception of arbitrary decision making
Moral	Recognizes the importance of values and attitudes in decision-making focus on the work Distributed and group decisions	Leveling out of leader/follower status Possible competing values of colleagues
Resonant	Focus on emotional development of staff members. Integrates the interrelated theories of emotional intelligence and resilience Attuned to the feelings of others and uses this empathy to move individuals in a positive direction	Enhanced emotional intelligence and resilience of all members of the school environment

cized because of its tendency to consider the leader as a hero, lacking some important leadership factors, having vague concepts and focus on certain transactional practices. The instructional leadership style has been criticized for assigning exceptionally high status to the leader, besides being task focused and authoritative in nature. Contrastingly, researchers often appreciate and advocate more adaptive and multiple oriented leadership styles. . . .

The basic features of an instructional leadership style include evolving a favorable environment for the teaching-learning process, having a mission in mind, and achieving a set objectives. . . .

Transformational leadership is aimed at bringing about a radical change in a school's existing state of affairs. . . .

Moral leadership is a more collaborative and distributed type of leadership, where importance is given to team work; however, cooperation and decisions are made on consensus. (Rehman, Kahn, and Waheed 2019, 139–41)

Turk and Wolfe discuss resonant leadership style:

The application of emotional intelligence and resilience theories by educational leaders has the potential to enhance the emotional intelligence and resilience of all members of the school environment. Resonant leaders are individuals who manage their own and others' emotions in ways that drive success. They are attuned to the feelings of the people they lead and use this empathy to move the individuals is a positive direction. In order to demonstrate resonant leadership, principals must successfully integrate the interrelated theories of emotional intelligence and resilience into their leadership style and practice. In order to achieve this goal, principals must first engage in the introspective process of identifying and cultivating their own emotional intelligence and resilience. By gaining insight into the symbiotic nature of these complementary concepts, principals gain insight into their ability to develop and sustain their resonant leadership. (Turk and Wolfe 2006, 150)

So, which leadership style is best? As in other educational areas, the style you choose will be determined by the situation. A combination of styles may also be appropriate and is usually warranted. Use one style as your overall guide, consider the pros and cons and the affect you want to have. Then vary your style when it becomes necessary or in order to reach a desired goal. The key is to be aware of your natural habit. For example, if you tend to be autocratic and top-down, find times that you can begin to be more democratic in your style. If your style is more relaxed and informal, find ways to communicate that you are focused on the task at hand. Or, when you see that conversations stop when you walk in, take steps to increase your emotional intelligence and put the tenets into practice. Find ways to solidify your connections with your colleagues.

What are your personal deal breakers? What are the things you will not tolerate under any circumstances? What situations require your immediate attention and intervention? Your compass has to be true and consistent. Do you require one thing from adults, but allow children or students to do another? Is the Arts Department a favorite, but the English Department always under the gun? Stealing, lying, by staff members? Treating children with disdain or their parents with disrespect? How about profanity? Whatever your personal deal breakers are, be consistent in your reaction. Be the example you wish to see in your colleagues or in your community. Actions always speak louder than words.

Chapter Seven

Discipline

Questions to consider as you read:

- What is your vision of an orderly school?
- Have you analyzed the effectiveness of your own theory of discipline?
- What is the developmental level of your students?
- Have teachers been trained in discipline techniques? What continuing training is in place?
- What are the particular or long-term disciplinary issues at your school?

This book would not be complete without a discussion on Discipline. There is no book or guide that can tell you exactly how to handle each student in your school so that they will do exactly what you expect them to do. How can we discuss discipline without discussing teachers? The discussion of discipline usually evolves into a discussion of classroom issues. This is unavoidable because classroom issues must be examined so that teachers have the opportunity to understand the logic behind what you are asking of them and what they are asking of students. The classroom is where the rubber meets the road. Any attempt to discuss discipline without discussing the teaching situation is futile. Principals who think they can control student behavior and student outcomes from the front office are kidding themselves.

Most principals were former teachers who were experts in discipline, so you probably have an extensive toolbox from which to draw to help teachers. Today, many of our teachers are novices at this point in our history, so they may need extensive coaching. In more than a few states, one can become a teacher simply by presenting his or her bachelor's degree and paying a fee to the state department of education. It is purely on-the-job training. Coaching can come from anyone (other teachers, a person who is solely hired to coach, or outside professionals). This chapter is meant to help administrators examine and clarify what they are asking of teachers and students.

What is your overall theory of discipline? Is it based on punishment and reward? On counseling? On making win-win deals with students?

Discipline is not punishment; it is a way of behaving in school. Is student discipline different today than it was when you were in school? Or have things changed so much that discipline is not really an issue? What were the disciplinary challenges of one hundred or fifty years ago, and have they changed? Are the discipline policies and procedures at your school effective? Do they work for every child? When you think of student discipline, do you see children standing with their backs against a wall at recess? Are they writing sentences over and over?

The disciplinary issues of today may be different, for example, instances of students bringing weapons to school have increased. But are today's children really different from how they were in the past? How have we made the necessary adjustments to our disciplinary procedure to be effective with the children of today? I am fairly certain that spanking has definitely come and gone permanently; at least in public schools. If spanking is still in effect in rural or private schools, I would urge any administrator, at any level, to immediately cease this practice.

Spanking may "work" on some children; however, by continuing the practice, you are opening yourself to personal and professional lawsuits. Even with "parental permission," if parents tell you they spank at home and allow you to do it too, you could go too far and hurt a child. Then, parents can change their mind and decide to take you to court.

So, what's a principal to do? There are so many things that can be done in the area of discipline. Number one, you must stop to consider, "What is the aim of student discipline?" Is it for punishment? Perhaps, but discipline is most effective when the administrator works from the viewpoint of discipline as a method to, in the end, change student behavior.

NEGATIVE AND POSITIVE REINFORCEMENT

Discipline may "feel like" punishment, to the student, and probably will work in the short term, but punishment is a negative reinforcer. It will only bring attention to the negative behavior and (unintentionally) reinforce it. Positive Reinforcement must be coupled with an emphasis on positive behavior. Focus on what you want the student to do, not what you want them to *not* do; or *stop* doing. In essence, the teacher will (virtually) ignore the wrong, bad, or inappropriate, behavior and "reward" the right, good, or appropriate behavior.

There are some children who are so used to being yelled at, hit, slapped, or ignored, that they have basically become addicted to negative reinforcement. All they have heard is "stop," "don't," "quit," or "no." So they act out in order to get the attention they crave. For these children, bad attention is better than no attention. This is why teachers claim to be counselor, nurse, and mom to their children. They really do take on these roles with their needy children; a huge challenge to do this *and* teach any subject.

Positive reinforcement can take the form of verbal comments such as, "You did a great job"; physical rewards such as, "You get to play an extra round of basketball"; or others, such as "Everyone gets a pencil when we all turn in homework." Rewards can be individual or class-wide; even school-wide.

Teachers should use positive verbal comments throughout the entire day. This encouragement becomes second nature to the teacher, and children, even high school students, never get tired of hearing the words. Find someone who is an expert on positive reinforcement and become trained along with your staff. It will pay off.

POSITIVE BEHAVIOR INTERVENTION

Encourage all teachers to use positive language in their classrooms and on their posts of class guidelines or class rules. Words such as *no*, *don't*, *stop*, or *quit* only bring the inappropriate behavior into focus and have a magnifying effect on undesirable behavior. Words have so much power. It has been said that the brain does not recognize a negative. Ask someone to do this: "Don't think of pink polka-dotted elephants." All they can think of is pink polka-dotted elephants. Place the focus, the emphasis, on what you *want* kids to do.

Table 7.1 is a sample class rules chart showing how any issue or situation calling for a negative injunction can be turned around—rephrased or reworded to make a positive statement. Enlist the help of your staff if you find you are stuck in the negative. With a little imagination, you can turn your entire school into a positive setting.

Model appropriate communication. Use good manners with children: "Please sit down." "Thank you for sitting so nicely." Corny? It really works.

The same positive behavior techniques also work with teachers. They may be "in on" what you are doing, but the effect is the same. You really have to work hard to defy a positive statement. Parents can also get in on the positive bandwagon. They may not realize how they are communicating with their children. People may simply need to be informed of a different way.

Table 7.1.

Issue	Instead of These Words (Negative)	Use These Words (Positive)
Gum chewing	Don't bring gum	We eat food at lunch. We keep our gum at home.
Hitting	Don't hit other children	Keep your hands to yourself.
Bullying	Stop bullying before it starts	Treat others with kindness and respect.

HOW DOES DISTRICT POLICY AFFECT YOUR SCHOOL?

Many school districts have formal policies and procedures for every disciplinary situation. The consequences (punishments) are well defined and outlined. Has a district policy ever stopped anyone from committing offences? No. Do kids stop writing on bathroom walls because it says so in the handbook? People (of all ages) are going to do what they are going to do. All a disciplinary policy does is inform you of what will, or could, happen if (when) you do one of these things. The district policy does make an attempt to treat every student fairly by codifying acts and punishments. It seeks to keep administrators from behaving in an "arbitrary and capricious" manner. However, students are all different, and when you consider the particular aspects of what was done, as well as the characteristics of each child, it may be difficult to adhere to policy.

The guidelines usually also come complete with a way to keep a (usually digital) record of what happened with all the details. Why are we keeping records on children who will make mistakes, sometimes repeating the same acts over and over? One reason is, when students move to another school or district, the staff at the new school won't be blindsided by what the student may do. On the other hand, you don't want to have the child become permanently labeled.

Maybe a change was just what the child needed. There are even varying results between teachers, subjects, environments, certainly among schools. Additionally, the child, and his family may need social services or counseling. No amount of positive behavior system will help fix a child who has been traumatized or abused or who has severe behavioral problems stemming from a metabolic cause. There are now new training programs that guide school personnel in techniques that include the consideration of trauma in a child's life and how to address behavioral issues that develop due to trauma.

So, use the code of conduct as a guide, but use your advanced education to make an "art" of discipline; administering discipline really is an art.

Personal Experience

At a large elementary school (K–5), I was in charge of virtually all discipline. I was the only assistant principal in a school of eight hundred-plus students. When I received a "referral" from a teacher, I would go to the classroom, sit in to see how the classroom was structured and get a feel for the teacher's expectations and observe the child. Then I would go over and ask the student to come with me. When we arrived at my office, I'd get his view of what had happened. The interview would involve what he or she could have done better and a discussion of what would happen "next time." I was extremely friendly, empathetic and displayed body language that showed I was really listening. I smiled a lot. These were real, genuine smiles because I just like kids—of all ages, even, or especially, the "bad" ones. In my role as administrator, I rarely got the opportunity to speak with children.

What I couldn't stand was a snippy, disrespectful child. Just my personal "thing." It took a lot of control to keep from snapping back (I too could be snippy). In any case, I would work with the child on math, or writing, or just let the child sit in silence for a while. Then I would escort the student back to class, after a time. It was just to give everyone a break to allow the situation to cool down. This usually worked.

The theory is that misbehaving students were not only disrupting the class, but actually stopping the learning. Not just stopping the learning, but stopping the teaching. That was when my personal motto of discipline was developed, "No one will stop me from teaching. No one will stop another student from learning." Maybe I had heard it somewhere, but it has helped me to focus on what's important—the learning must go on. Not "I must punish this child." In addition, keeping the focus on learning removes the discipline from being an indictment on the child's character and changes it to being a support of the student's education.

What about consistent and continual behavior infractions? This requires a bit of detective work. Talk to the child's teacher (all of them if possible) and make an effort to find out exactly what's going on. Arrange a team meeting to discuss the child. Does the child have what she needs to succeed? Is the student attempting to distract from the fact that he is struggling with the material? Is it a self-confidence issue? Is this behavior occurring only in the classroom—or is it everywhere the child goes? A thousand other variables could be the problem. If you could arrange a meeting with the teacher(s) first, then with the parents, you could put your heads together to find out what is going on. Without really thinking about what's happening and possibly why, and simply doling out punishments based on the code of conduct, the behavior probably will not change. Use the scientific method: develop a hypothesis, institute an intervention, evaluate results. Start again if the desired effect doesn't occur.

While using the computer or app-based disciplinary tracking program, attempt to enter as many details about the incident as possible. The basics will be prompted by the program (when, where, who, what, etc.). The reports that are promulgated by the system will help to give you insights about where the child has issues. Patterns are usually apparent, after you've seen the student eight times in two weeks. This will definitely require a team meeting.

Avoid being the only adult to discipline a child who constantly has issues. It will seem (mostly to parents) that you have a personal vendetta or that you are "out to get" the child. In addition, you need more than one point of view. All of this takes a tremendous amount of time, but if you will "front-load" your discipline plan, do the required work in advance, it will reduce what you have to do later on in the year as these problems tend to pile up.

SCHOOL CODE OF CONDUCT OR "UNITY IN THE COMMUNITY"

Every school has its particular set of circumstances that require tweaking of the district plan. Whatever your challenges are, whatever you and your staff wish to see in your school will be included in the school code of conduct. This plan is much less detailed and is tailored for your school. Many schools repeat the "top three" rules each morning, just as a reminder; a subconscious guide for everyone to follow. Words have power. "Treat everyone with kindness." Call everyone by their right name." "Finish all assignments." Use broad terms that cover many situations. This way you will promote unity in expectations. The entire staff needs to be in on the "deal breakers," the nonnegotiables. It is really difficult for everyone, parents, teachers, children, when one teacher allows gum, let's say, and another teacher doesn't.

MANAGE YOUR EMOTIONS (AND YOUR TEACHERS AND ADMINISTRATORS TOO)

We all have emotions, of course, and some people's emotions are closer to the surface than others. Having emotions is what makes us human. Start with yourself. Your goal is to appear calm and cool in *all* situations. People are counting on you to be the rock. This is not to say that you cannot express grief, joy, or disappointment. A principal can in fact model the *management* of emotions. Express what you are feeling, but quickly get back to your primary mission. We all felt so sad when _____, let's get back to learning. Or I almost ran around the halls because I was so excited that _____ but I think I'll save that for my evening jog.

Most of all, manage your emotions during disciplinary actions. If you need to take a moment to cool off, ask the student to sit quietly while you complete paperwork. Avoid, at all costs, placing a call to the student's parent while you are "hot," You want to sound like a true professional. Your anger *will* come across over the phone. Put a smile on your face, ask the parent if it is a good time to talk, then ask for a conference. Ask if they would prefer to speak in person. You have to be truly sorry to have to report that their child was involved in ____ that happened in the ____. Send the paperwork home only after you have made a verbal contact with the parent. Even if you had to leave a message, some contact has been made. If you will put yourself in the parent's shoes, your empathy will guide you to do the right thing.

Parents are doing the best they can. Not what *you* think is the best, but what only they know how and what to do. Sometimes educators can be instrumental in "training" parents in child behavior and child psychology. Parents want the best for their children, some could use a little guidance, and will appreciate it.

LONG-TERM INFLUENCE/EFFECT

When administering discipline, educators must consider the short-term and long-term effects of what they do. Speaking to children, with the expectation that they can understand, is a good first step to allowing them to consider their own life. If the student has no clue about what you are saying, then take a step toward the developmental or emotional level where the student can comprehend what you want to convey.

This is especially true with middle and high school students. Developmental levels vary greatly from student to student, and educators need to tailor their communication as they speak with each one. Most mild discipline can be handled by the teacher or the teacher/grade level team, with little long-term effect (staying inside for today's recess). Other discipline techniques can have longer-term damaging effects. The worst is, of course, physical punishment (such as spanking or excessive physical stress—doing multiple pushups, etc.).

Next worse is assigning extra and excessive classwork as punishment (look up fifty words in the dictionary and write the meaning, write one hundred times I will not . . .). Why are these damaging? Learning is not a punishment. It may not always be fun, but it should not be seen as punishment. Suspending classroom privileges can work, but the child should not have to do this more than a few consecutive days.

Spending time with the student can work—as long as the focus is on academics. Many principals ask students to sit in their office while they complete classwork. This gives you a chance to have a discussion about what is going on with the student. Your aim is to help the child to see that off-task behavior has a direct effect on achievement in the classroom. The only problem with having students in your office is that the principal's office can be a busy place; children tend to listen to adult conversations, and have a good old time being with the grownups. Being in the principal's office can be a positive reinforcing event. In the child's mind, misbehaving could allow entrance to a special place where his craving for attention can be satisfied.

Some teachers may view the principal as the person who will "get students to behave." They may become stuck in a reporting mode, where they are basically repeatedly saying, "Look what he did," and releasing the child to you. The teacher may not internalize the fact that as the adult in the room, they really do have control over their classroom and have the ability to address problems themselves. Also, they may not have considered team mates or colleagues they can enlist for help. Your job is to guide the teacher to get into the problem-solution mode and explore options for behavioral intervention.

School-wide discipline policies will work only if everyone knows about them. Students, parents, and teachers must be on the same page. This especially applies to teachers, who are the primary contact with students. If your school has a strong set of widely known discipline policies, you are definitely ahead of the game. However, knowing the policies and procedures is different from actually instituting them. People may "agree" with the policies, but as human beings, we tend to revert to what we knew before we became teachers. People tend to draw from the discipline they experienced when they were in school, how their teachers did it, and how they interpreted and internalized appropriate discipline. Conversely, people may remember what was done to them and vow never to do the same.

So, teacher training is needed for schools that lack a traditional, dyed-in-the-wool discipline policy; additionally, it is needed for schools where a crop of new teachers enters your building each year. If you are in this latter category, it would be best to begin with one or two nonnegotiable items, such as a policy on chewing gum or handing out candy or whatever you and the current staff agree is the primary issue. Make sure that the policy that you have chosen is well defined. Take, for example, "Respect everyone." This goal is a good one, but it is too nebulous. "Respect everyone" might be better articulated as "Call everyone by their right name." Much more specific.

In a school where there are many problems, focusing on one objective may seem like a drop in the bucket, but you have to begin somewhere. Any more than one or two goals at a time will be overwhelming for everyone. Yes, you will need to deal with other issues, such as fighting, incomplete schoolwork, and so on, but to change the culture, changes need to be instituted and focused on one at a time, in small doses.

After the goal is identified, repeating it daily will be necessary. We are dealing with children and young adults. When students see and understand that the staff is on the same page, thinking the same way, they will fall in line. Will there be outlying children? Of course, but the effect of the majority is what you are after; positive peer pressure. No school (or business or organization) can function or be successful if everyone is doing what they want, how they want, when they want, on a regular basis.

DISCIPLINE TEAMS (GRADE OR SUBJECT LEVEL)

One of the most effective discipline systems involves teacher teams. It is a system in which teachers in the same grade or subject have gotten together and decided how discipline will be handled.

For example, third grade teachers have decided that completing work is their number one issue. Students who do not finish assignments (due to playing around, talking, etc.) are required to finish the work during class recess. Usually, school days are structured where teachers plan lessons or have lunch while students are involved in recreation. Once students realize that their teacher cares enough to give up their own free time to help them, the number of students who need to "stay in" gradually diminishes to almost zero. Although the children see this as punishment, it is not. It is helping the child to realize that time is of the essence and maximum effort is required of them.

A problem can occur when one or two teachers don't agree with this "gift" of their time. If team members can be convinced that it truly is a short-term situation (usually three to four weeks) and that it will work in the long run, they will find that their classroom becomes more orderly and that there's not a daily struggle to get children to do what you are asking them to do. This can also be difficult when there is a teacher union involved. Staff members may complain that there is not enough time to plan lessons, and so on.

This procedure can also work in conjunction with a school-wide discipline procedure where one person is designated (and paid) to be in charge of students who display "second-level" behaviors (fighting, extreme disrespect to others, extremely disruptive behavior). These students are removed from the classroom for a day, or the remainder of the day. Where do they go? They go to the specially designed classroom where the goal is to consider their behavior and complete classwork. The programs are known as in-school suspension or intervention. Students bring their classroom assignments with them, eat lunch together, and work on their own. The aim is to help students realize what they are missing due to their misbehavior. The teacher will monitor the students and is trained to recognize the students' motivation and how they interact with other students and the teacher.

Many students who find themselves in this situation are displaying these behaviors due to emotional or academic issues. Many have been referred to special services and are waiting for an evaluation. Some simply become caught up in another student's issues and end up reacting in the wrong way. This is where counseling comes in. Counseling can take the form of a simple conversation between the student and the intervention teacher or sessions with a professional counselor and involving the family.

With older students, especially minority or poor students, discipline problems can contribute to the school-to prison pipeline. These students are caught (through no fault of their own) in a pattern of arriving at school unprepared due to a variety of issues: there may be a language barrier, a lack of supplies, minimal background knowledge of the subject, gaps in knowledge, lack of teacher awareness and tolerance, or teacher or administrative bias. The students (they are all children; some are as tall as you, but they are still children) tend to act, react, and end up being removed from the very place that can provide them help.

Teacher training is vitally necessary in this circumstance. Staff training should involve:

- Setting a welcoming environment: The power of a smile and welcoming body language.
- Setting expectations: Consistent throughout the subject area classes.
- Setting grading policies (especially the no-grade below a 50): This is a very hot topic that makes teaching professionals uncomfortable or even angry. The principal and teacher teams should research the issue and seriously consider how this can be a logical technique for teachers, if not for the entire school, in homework and final test policies.
- Setting interventions: Talk privately, reduce attention to the noncompliant behavior, display positive emotions, inquire about the student's emotions, develop a solution with the student. Place the student (and teacher) back in a neutral position.
- Resources and procedures: Policies for students who display constant and continual problems (refer them to counseling, special services, wraparound (family) social services.

In under-funded schools, meet with your district personnel to explore the redistribution of resources so that you can meet your goals. Although most programs that come with money have tightly outlined qualifications of how the money is to be used, there are ways to creatively (not illegally) use these funds to meet your goals. Closely examine the qualifications of these budgetary items, meet with upper-level personnel, and try to get what you need through communication and compromise.

The good news is that our society is recognizing these issues and many schools are coming around to the community school concept. Community schools provide full-service social workers and basic health screenings for everyone in the community.

PROGRESSIVE DISCIPLINE

Progressive discipline is a procedure whereby the punishment levels up as the behavior gets worse or more constant. Seems like a solid, logical idea. Why doesn't this work? The district code of conduct says to do this. A student goes from one, to three, to five days suspension. Then long-term suspension where the student is assigned to an alternative school and does not return for the remainder of the school year.

The district's code of conduct is a *guide* for administrators. With few exceptions (weapons or threats of harm), the administrator has latitude in how to classify and deal with infractions. Keep in mind, the more laws you have, the more criminals you make. Progressive discipline leads the child to see that their situation is hopeless. It makes students focus on inappropriate behavior. Anything that you are trying "not" to do, you will end up doing. Progressive discipline helps the situation to become hopeless (suspended 1, 3, 5, 7 days) and ends up rewarding the behavior instead of extinguishing it. The only people helped by progressive discipline is the teacher, because the child is out of his or her immediate supervision. But what happens when the child comes back? The child is more behind than ever, having missed instruction, and is discouraged, disoriented, and displaced. Maybe the items in their desk are gone. It is a disaster.

In lieu of suspension, work with the parents and strongly encourage their attendance (or the attendance of another relative/caring adult) with the child, even for a few hours. If the child needs, and can only function with that degree of support, there are other issues involved. This is where referral to professional services comes in. No teacher should feel alone in the situation, with no one to help.

On the other hand, encouraging teacher teams to work together on discipline can be extremely effective. Maybe teachers are willing to "exchange" students. Doesn't seem fair—shouldn't all teachers be able to teach all students? Perhaps, but we are not talking about fairness, we are talking about effectiveness. Wouldn't you change physicians if your doctor wasn't a good fit for you? A teacher change is one of the last options that should be available to any student. The child could get the idea that running away from problems is appropriate.

In any case, you, as the administrator, must avoid being the one person to go to for discipline problems. If you encourage staff members to bring all discipline issues to you, you have done two things: crippled the teacher's ability to take charge of his or her room, and turned yourself into the big bad discipline person. Discipline can (and will) take all your time, especially in a school with a large student population. You will have a steady stream (and a waiting room) of discipline cases. For most administrators, this simply will not work. If you find yourself in this situation, balance it with humor and get involved in positive school activities while working to change it.

TEACHER PERSONALITY

Within the framework of having consistent discipline policies in the school, there is much room for each teacher to be themselves, to express their uniqueness and have fun in the classroom. If you observe the teachers in your building, you will probably notice that the teachers who express themselves, so that students feel they know them, have fewer disciplinary issues. Teachers who express a genuine regard for the welfare of their students have the most success in getting students to comply, learn, and engage. Notice the verb *express*. Most teachers do have a genuine positive regard; they just don't understand the importance of *expressing* it.

Just to be clear, expressing your personality cannot include having your own rules at cross purposes with the school rules. This is why choosing one, two, or three nonnegotiable rules for your school is important. Leave room for the expression of unique personality.

"No student will keep another child from learning, and no child will keep a teacher from teaching." This wording helps refocus everyone. It covers just about every possible situation. Every time a teacher has to stop to ask a student to remove her gum or stop drawing on someone else's paper, the lesson is interrupted, disrupting the flow of learning. These seconds add up. Students are busy. In the typical elementary school day, there are at least eight times where they must stop what they are doing and transition to another activity.

These stops, starts, and transitions (putting things away, lining up, walking to the next class) add up to approximately sixty minutes of instruction missed per day. If you add to that all the micro-misbehaviors that are addressed, the teacher has a very limited window in which to teach and reteach the subject at hand.

In high schools, it is much the same. In a traditional six-hour schedule with five minutes to walk to each class, lunch, opening and closing, teachers need at least five minutes at the beginning and five minutes at the end of *each* period for housekeeping. The more time spent addressing infractions, the less time there is for learning. Not only do teachers resent interruptions, but students do as well. Teachers need to make sure their teaching techniques encourage students to *want* to learn.

Peer pressure will encourage misbehaving students to get with the program and stop interrupting. If there's nothing special going on but copying words and definitions, kids will actually look forward to (and may even stimulate and inspire) the misbehavior of others, just for a break; a bit of fun. Great lessons (interesting, not necessarily fun) usually help to extinguish or minimize misbehavior.

Below are a few particular issues discussed according to your assigned school level.

Elementary Level

How do you discipline a forty-pound pre-K student? A six-foot-tall fifth grader? In an elementary school, it is for certain you will handle both, and in the same day. Pre-K and kindergarten teachers are usually experts in disciplining their students. The same goes for first- and second-grade experts. Teachers who have trouble with students on a consistent basis, may not be knowledgeable about current theories of behavior and interventions. These young students usually want to please the teacher and may do whatever their teacher is asking of them. If not, there are usually other issues that must be addressed. Meet with the teachers to discuss options for interventions for the student and/or her family.

Although these small children can be challenging and inspire a good amount of frustration in any teacher, we must avoid at all costs, physical punishment. Standing in a corner for a short time is about the extent of physical intervention that can be allowed. Standing is a way to address, to some extent, a need for physical movement, a way to remove the child from the immediate situation, while at the same time, the child is still in the classroom environment. It is a way to keep them out of the hall, where the teacher has no idea of what is going on, and can be seen as a treat for the students. Even standing in a corner can be seen as punishment by the student. It is all in the way it is done. Saying, "Would you come over here with me?" is different than "Get over there in that corner." The adults in the room cannot use their physical and psychological power in a way that diminishes the humanity of the child.

What about more subtle problems such as talking too much, or interrupting others? These are habits that children develop over time, usually at home. Talking is not at all a bad thing. Children can understand logic and are able to discuss the "why" of a situation. These are habits that you can help the child to unlearn or redirect. As with any person, if you can privately talk about habits with the child, you will have greater success in getting your point across. Start with a "have you noticed" statement. Tell the child what you've noticed and try to get the child to admit that the habit is one that would be good to change. Talking is not a bad thing. Have the child name five things that are good about talking.

With older students, have them name five professions in which someone who is good at talking can excel. Always find a positive aspect to the habit that the child is displaying. Even aggression has a place—sports, for example. With children, helping them to see that there is a time and place for everything helps them to see how they fit in the world.

Keep academic activities for learning, not for punishment. Asking students to write one hundred sentences doesn't help their impression of school being a place for learning. Many students disengage because they simply cannot do the work, so their self-esteem plummets. As soon as they are old enough, they simply drop out, physically. Psychologically, they dropped out long before.

The aim of discipline is to correct behavior, not change their personality. Discipline in any group setting is necessary. Why? So that the organization can function effectively and so that everyone involved can get what they need from it, to realize their individual goals and dreams.

Keep the essence of the child, but control it so they can have room to learn and grow. It is obvious that second-grade boys will have a degree of rambunctious behavior. In fact, girls and boys at times demonstrate a need for (sometimes extreme) movement. There are all types of children, the artistic ones, the quiet introspective children, the students who seem to crave attention—all kinds, just like there are all types of adults. Children are adults in the making. They have particular needs as they negotiate the world and go through stages as they mature. Learning to accept the stage they are in is part of being an effective educator. So, as you find yourself in situations regarding discipline, consider the developmental level as well as the child's individual personality before administering discipline; even where there are strict guidelines in place. If you can follow up with students that you have seen for disciplinary reasons, it will help to positively reinforce the things that you've discussed with the student. There is something special about being with the principal, in her office, and having a conversation that helps children to see that you are on their side and are working for their good. Most children end up with a view of you that is very different from when they only see you in the hall or in the cafeteria for a short amount of time. Just a simple smile and wave helps to solidify their view of you as another caring adult in their lives.

Visiting the child's classroom might seem like it would be helpful. In reality, in a child's mind, you are the "heavy" in the building. Some children may straighten up and fly right while you are there, then upon your exit, immediately revert to the inappropriate behavior. Most children are not mature enough to see their classroom behavior as problematic. They are still on the "big bad wolf" developmental stage. This is why teams of classroom teachers who handle discipline are more effective than using the administrator on a routine basis for discipline.

Middle School

Middle school is a developmentally sensitive time. It is the time when children *continue*, not *begin*, their journey into adulthood. They have been on this journey since childhood, and many of their habits and personality traits are deeply ingrained; therefore, they may be difficult to change.

Physical and hormonal changes in students of this age are the source of many of the situations or problems they find themselves immersed in. Middle school students' bodies are rapidly changing and their brains are expanding. Students of this age are beginning to choose their friends, hobbies, and interests. Differing rates of mental and physical maturity present a challenge to teachers and administrators. They seem to grow up overnight. The psychological changes and the transition to adulthood prompts administrators to react much differently with these middle schoolers than with other ages.

For example, you might "ask" a middle school student if you can contact the student's parents. Addressing the student's developing sense of agency can instill a sense that, as an almost-adult, the student needs to begin to realize that actions have consequences. Inquire if the student has a counselor or if another adult's participation might be needed or desired in developing a solution to whatever is going on.

In other words, being less autocratic and more democratic with the student works for the good of all. Some middle school students already have a history with the social services department; they have had to "grow up" fast due to family circumstances or familial responsibilities. Consider that the child may already feel grown up because of having had to function as one at home.

On the other hand, there are many middle schoolers who will respond to traditional middle school punishments such as getting detention, or performing extra community service activities, instead of getting into a deep discussion with an adult. They are just not ready; or their parents have provided for their psychological needs and support.

With middle school students, keep a light hand when documenting their issues. Because of their development being in flux, they are more likely to become involved in something fairly serious, but after they've been called on it, will be "scared straight." Most likely they won't see you again. So, why put something on their permanent record that may be a one time situation, something that doesn't reflect their character or that could be damaging to them as a high school student? If it occurs again, you can always go back to enter it.

Middle school discipline still involves helping kids to accurately see themselves and others, to become aware of their effect on other people. It involves shaping young lives so they can survive and thrive as they move into high school and beyond.

High School

High school is where records really matter. High schools have almost become what colleges used to be. Advanced subjects (algebra and chemistry) that were once taught in college are taught to high school freshmen. There is more pressure than ever for students to be successful in high school. They need to not only graduate, but also have firm plans about what is next. High school students are expected to know what they want and be able to take steps needed to reach their goals.

Freshmen come in wide-eyed and afraid. Many are still negotiating the issues that some middle schoolers may have already mastered. Most are disorganized and still seeking what they haven't yet found in life. Incoming high schoolers could be, and probably are, struggling with a variety of things. Hence, the Freshman Academy that most schools have designed. Freshman students are usually semi-sequestered within the school. They have their own set of teachers, classes, and a dedicated counselor. As the year progresses, they branch out to become fairly independent as sophomore year approaches.

Discipline at this age is also as varied as the students are. Although required by law to attend, a significant number of students are in school because they want better lives and can see how doing well in school leads to doing well in life. Others are there because there is literally nowhere else to go, being too young to drive or work, or because of truancy laws, or just to bide time until they are old enough to drop out. Some are actively in business—selling illegal substances—or are involved in other unsavory activities. Some may be helping out in a family business as well. The students who are at school but have no idea why or who don't see a path to success in life make up the majority of discipline problems in high schools. There is a path for everyone; the administrator has to work with counselors and other mentors to help students see the possibilities for their lives.

All in all, the typical high schooler wants to come to school. Graduating from high school is not only expected, but it is seen as key to a basically successful life; even if college is not an option. Kids want to come to school, but there must be something to come to school for.

Many students come to school to feed their special interest. It could be drama, music, socializing with peers, athletics, advanced academics, or other special offerings of the school. The problem is with students who, because of language barriers, transportation, financial hardship, or other issues, cannot get involved with their passion. It is truly sad when a student can only struggle through basic classes in English, math, science, and social studies without something particular they can excel in.

Without something that makes them feel special, students may conclude there is not much use in sitting through the required courses. Even students that are not struggling need something that stokes their particular interest. For many students, these extracurricular activities make school worth showing up for. Going to the cooking class and making cream puffs makes biology worth sitting through.

Without an extensive list of extracurriculars for high school students, "something for everyone," discipline problems are likely to occur. But even with all the classes and extracurriculars to choose from, discipline problems will always be on the menu. Having a strong code of conduct will help the administrator to be fair.

The school code of conduct mirrors the civil and criminal laws of our nation and of the states. You violate *this* law—*that* happens. Students of this age have been in school for at least ten years. They know the rules. There are few "accidents" when it comes to infractions of the rules. At this age, bending the rules and their consequences does more harm than good. The administrator has to be firm in administering consequences.

Progressive discipline only works when the steps are clear and distinct. High school students are able to process words, think on a higher level, and see what's coming next. Unfortunately, social structures are not always in place to support the young person who is struggling. Your best helpers in this regard would be a strong counseling center or mentorship program to help students who still struggle with making appropriate choices.

At the high school level, your discussions with students should focus on problem solving—informing students about available services and local, state, and federal laws. They need to know there are very real consequences to their actions. Encourage them to choose the right friends, let some old friends go, be brave enough to chart their own course, and to find something they are good at and can do to actually make a living. Help students to identify areas where they are strong, what their interests are, and how they plan to get to their dream. Sounds like counseling? It is exactly like counseling. It is a little late to attempt to discipline a high school student into doing the right thing. As all human beings must do, they must choose how they are going to spend their time on earth. With some help from their own village, which includes you, they are likely to make a choice that is good, not only for them, but for the entire community.

Conclusion

In this book I have advocated for principals who may have limited support and mentorship from their district. Although all professionals have a duty to seek mentors and help from their colleagues, I believe that well-written books can also help. It is my hope that you will add this book to your professional book collection. I also encourage teachers, principals, and other school leaders to explore leadership through reading about and observing leadership practices in the business community. Although school administrators are paid far less, we have the same responsibilities as business leaders. We are also working with adults who have the desire to be effective and to succeed.

In the end, although we can use leadership theory to improve our schools, our final product is not a new car or an improved website. Our unique product is a whole, functioning, beautiful person who will either be an asset or a burden; or, like all of us as we exist in this world, a mix of the two. That is what makes education leadership unique.

I hope I have succeeded in providing practical suggestions to equip new principals with the tools to enhance their practice. May you have a long and fruitful career in school leadership.

References

Bacal, Robert. N.d. "Understanding Informal Leaders in an Organization (and Benefiting from Them)." Leader Today. http://leadertoday.org/articles/informalleadersunderstanding.htm.

Bagwell, Jack L. 2014. "Exploring the Leadership Practices of Elementary School Principals through a Distributed Leadership Framework: A Case Study." *Educational Leadership and Administration, Teaching and Program Development* 30 (March 2019): 83–103.

Cutler, Alan. 2014. *Leadership Psychology: How the Best Leaders Inspire Their People*. London: Kogan Page.

Frances, O. B. and Oluwatoyin, F. C. (2019). "Principals' Personnel Characteristic Skills: A Predictor of Teachers' Classroom Management in Ekiti State Secondary School." *International Journal of Educational Leadership and Management*, 7(1), 72–103.

Intercultural Development Research Association (IDRA). 2019. *Equity-Based Framework for Achieving Integrated Schooling: A Framework for School Districts and Communities in Designing Racially and Economically Integrated Schools*, ED591358. https://www.idraeacsouth.org/wp-content/uploads/2018/12/Equity-Based-Framework-for-Achieving-Integrated-Schooling-112718.pdf.

Jones, Jeff. 2004. *Management Skills in Schools: A Resource for School Leaders*. London: Sage.

LeaderToday.org. N.d. Leadership Resource Center. http://leadertoday.org/faq/informalleader.htm

Rehman, A-U., M. I. Kahn, and Z. Waheed. 2019. "School Heads' Perceptions about Their Leadership Styles." *Journal of Education and Educational Development* 6 (1): 138–53.

Schmidt, Eric, Jonathan Rosenberg, and Alan Eagle. 2019. *Trillion Dollar Coach: The Leadership Playbook of Silicon Valley's Bill Campbell*. New York: HarperBusiness.

Stafford, Delia, and Valerie Hill-Jackson. 2016. *Better Principals, Better Schools: What Star Principals Know, Believe, and Do*. Charlotte, NC: Information Age Publishing.

Stein, S., and H. E. Book. 2011. *The EQ Edge: Emotional Intelligence and Your Success*. Third edition. Mississauga, ON: John Wiley & Sons, Canada.

Study.com. 2016. "Informal Leadership: Definition & Explanation." study.com/academy/lesson/informal-leadership-definition-lesson-quiz.html.

Turk, Ellen W., and Zora M. Wolfe. 2019."Principal's Perceived Relationship between Emotional Intelligence, Resilience, and Resonant Leadership throughout Their Career." *International Journal of Educational Leadership Preparation* 14 (1): 147–69.

About the Author

Margaret Carter received a BA in elementary education from Central State University (now the University of Central Oklahoma), an MA in reading from the University of Central Oklahoma, and an MA in education administration from UCO as well. Mrs. Carter taught in Oklahoma City Public Schools for fifteen years and worked as an administrator for fourteen years. She has taught students of all grade and ability levels from first grade through high school, and she served as an elementary school principal and a high school assistant principal. The schools were located in inner-city, rural, and suburban communities. She has also tutored students in Midwest City–Del City schools. Currently she continues her work through her consulting company, Rosander Education Consulting. Contact information: margaretcarterok@gmail.com; (405)924-0827.

www.ingramcontent.com/pod-product-compliance
Lightning Source LLC
Chambersburg PA
CBHW021215240426
43672CB00026B/327